Motivating With Sales Contests:
The Complete Guide to Motivating Your Telephone Professionals with Contests That Produce Record-Breaking Results

Including 79 Contests You Can Run Right Now

David L. Worman

This book was printed on recycled paper, and saved over nine trees.

Published By Business By Phone Inc.
5301 S. 144th St.
Omaha, NE 68137 USA
(402)895-9399

Dedication

I dedicate this book to the people who truly gave of themselves to make this book possible: my family. You selflessly gave up your time with me, encouraged me endlessly, and supported me unconditionally. To my loving wife and best friend, Kathy, my daughters, Michelle and Jackie, and my son, Danny. I love you.

In Loving Memory

I write this book in memory of my father, Philip H. Worman, Jr. (1916-1992), who, throughout his life, by example showed me the meaning and taught me the importance of true people skills. Without this special gift this book and the events leading up to, and contributing to it, would not have been possible. Thank you, Dad, for what has always been, and will always be, the predominant factor in any and all growth of my professional accomplishments.

With Special Thanks To . . . .

My secretary, Kathi Squire, who gave countless hours of her own time to take all my thoughts on tape (and in longhand) and type them into reality.

All of the creative people who submitted contest ideas for this book, exemplifying the wide diversity of talented people in the fields of telemarketing and telesales.

Art Sobczak, the publisher of this book, for the opportunity to make a dream come true. Thank you for your assistance, encouragment, and most of all, your belief in me.

Table of Contents

Chapter 8. 79 Contests That Work *(continued)*

Chapter 8. 79 Contests That Work *(continued)*

A Final Note From Dave Worman

Foreword

What You Should Know About Dave Worman

By Art Sobczak

Whenever I pick up a book, it's always more enjoyable if I know of the author, or have heard him speak, so that from the beginning of the book, I have a feel for the voice, the feelings . . . . the person behind the words. I love being able to hear that voice speaking to me as I turn the pages. And that's my purpose for writing this for you — to help you know Dave Worman. Because doing so will help you appreciate even more the fine journey you're about to take.

I first met Dave when he attended one of my Telesales Rep College training seminars. I'd like to tell you I remember everyone who attends my programs, but speaking before thousands per year, that's not possible. Dave stood out, though.

I remember this guy, who, although in appearance and actions was very businesslike, had this "aw' shucks" demeanor, and incredibly intense sincerity when speaking. His was a genuine interest in what you had to say. You know the type . . . . the people you warm up to right away . . . . the kind of person you'd like to have as a neighbor to swap stories with over the back fence.

And the enthusiasm! I remember touching on a few points during the seminar, that for most people, would elicit a nod of the head and a few notes. Dave, on the other hand, would get this *"Oh my gosh, this is great!"*-look on his face (at times even saying it), and then wildly scribble notes in his book.

His comments also burned an impression in my mind. Always contributing, adding great tips about what he does for his people to help them grow. I remember thinking, "Here's a guy who really, truly, practices what all managers should have as their goal: making the development of their people their number one objective."

After the program a few months had passed. I thought of Dave when I saw his photo and an article on sales contests in a magazine. I was pleasantly surprised to see him getting some national exposure, sharing his knowledge and enthusiasm so he could enhance the lives of others.

Shortly before Christmas, 1991, Dave contacted me with a training question. The conversation was enjoyable and lively, bouncing to a number of subjects (as it does when you're talking with someone who gives you that feeling they enjoy talking to YOU, and also has lots of interesting things to share), when we both realized we were scheduled to speak to the same local chapter of the American Telemarketing Association (on different dates) in the Spring. Dave was to speak on his area of expertise: sales contests.

How This Book Was Conceived

I shared that at one time I had dabbled with the idea of putting together a book of contests, since so many people called my office over the years asking if such a resource was available. Dave agreed that there was a definite need, based on the response he got at presentations. Then he said it: "I've got enough ideas to fill a book." I spontaneously responded, "So let's do it!"

I only wish I could have seen Dave's face as I tossed out ideas to him, and with his adorable boyish manner, was seeing a dream materialize before his eyes! The agreement for this book was hammered out on that one phone call, and the work began.

In working with Dave through the months I came to know him better, firming up my belief that he is one of the most genuine humans you'll ever run across. His dedication to his people, his family, and to his values is real. He shares these same values and feelings with you in this book.

In editing and reading through the initial drafts many (many!) times, I can say without reservation that Dave speaks from experience, and the feelings flow from deep in his heart. The enthusiasm that shouts at you from these pages is sincere, not because he looks better as a manager when his people are motivated, but because THEY develop as people. And that makes him happier than any accolade.

Dave amazes me with his knowledge and experience regarding contests. Regardless of how many times I sat down and edited, and then proofread these chapters, I still couldn't force myself to *just look* at the words for possible typos; I became absorbed in the insightful advice and experiences Dave shares.

As you read these chapters, hear the voice of a friend you've yet to meet . . . . . someone who's talking to you, one-on-one. Because, just as he's interested in seeing his own people develop, he's also concerned with ensuring that you'll be more successful as a manager, learning from his experiences, and those of others.

Laugh along with him, lean forward and listen closely when he tells you to avoid the mistakes he's made, USE these ideas, and most of all, as Dave so often states and exhibits, **get excited!**

Congratulations on investing in your success, and that of your people. Enjoy!

Art Sobczak
President, Business By Phone Inc.
Omaha, NE

Introduction

Why I Wrote this Book, and How to Use It

My objective with this book is to help you, my fellow manager, create an environment in which it is easier to help your people develop. Essentially, to help you motivate your employees. Which, in turn, makes your job (and theirs) easier, more fun, and makes you look better as a manager.

And you'll accomplish all of this by implementing successful contests in your telephone environment.

You, as I, know that it's difficult to work on the telephone, all day, every day. And it's no wonder: the redundancy of call after call, the relentless rejection, and the overall roller coaster ride through peaks and valleys associated with telephone sales has the potential to adversely affect even the most positive individuals. Just by listening to many of you at the conventions and association meetings I speak at, I am convinced that the burnout levels (and subsequent turnover) in telesales/telemarketing takes a back seat to no other industry. And that makes our jobs as managers more difficult.

Believe me, I can relate, because I've been there, I am there, and I will continue to be there with you .... fighting the same battles you're waging day-after-day. I share in your anxiety, pain, confusion, frustration, fear, and intense effort that is associated with keeping our employees happy, enthusiastic, and performing at their highest level of potential.

I received my first view of the mountains we, as managers, must scale during my first week in telemarketing. Back in 1986, as an Assistant Telemarketing Manager for *USA TODAY*, I sensed that something needed to be done to motivate those people, or I wouldn't likely be around too long (or at least I wouldn't be happy with what I was doing). Therefore, applying my longstanding belief that "A happy employee is a more productive employee," and that constructive fun in the workplace enhances the attitudes (and therefore, production) of employees, I decided to find new ways to motivate.

After much tinkering, I latched onto the best answer: contests. When I ran contests, I found my people were more energized, they sold more, and ultimately, they stuck around longer.

After moving to Manager of Corporate Telemarketing for Diebold, Inc., I applied the same beliefs and systems to business-to-business telesales — with equally pleasing results.

In this book, I share my "secrets" with you. You'll learn:

- which contests work best, and why;

- how long contests should last, and when you should run them;

- how to determine contest production goals;

- what you should award to contest winners;

- how to avoid the inevitable post-contest letdown,

and many other techniques I've fine-tuned over the years. You'll also be the benefactor of my rough times, fellow manager. The scars are still fresh from many ideas-gone-sour. I'll help you avoid these costly and painful mistakes.

And finally, you'll see 79 proven contests you can lift from these pages, just as you would recipes from a cookbook, to use today in your own office.

How to Use this Book
As enticing as it might seem to dive right into Chapter 8, which details the 79 Contests You Can Use, I caution you: **don't** . . . . until you've read the other chapters. I don't know if you're like

me, but I'm the kind of guy who doesn't read the instructions when I try to assemble my kids' toys, or get a new electronic toy of my own. But time and again, I regret it afterward, because I wind up going to the instructions anyway, and it takes me more time to correct what I messed up. Don't let that happen to you with your contests. Sure, the contests alone will work. But, by going through the other chapters first, you will dramatically reduce the chance of avoidable errors, along with the accompanying grief, loss of time, and potentially lingering feelings of negativism by your people.

So please, fellow manager, read through these chapters. Highlight the points. Dog-ear the pages. Let this be your guide, as it has for me for so many years. Then select the contests you want to use, and adapt them to your (and your sales reps') personality, environment, industry, and objectives.

An Invitation

After implementing these ideas, undoubtedly you'll experience success. I hope you'll let me know what you've done and how you've done it. I'd like the opportunity to congratulate you . . . . not just for what you've accomplished, but for what you've done for your people. And perhaps your ideas and contests could be included in a potential sequel to this book.

Or, if you are in the same situation I was when I first started in telemarketing, you might find some of this overwhelming, or perhaps need personal assistance. If so, I invite you to discuss that with me as well, as I'm available to aid companies in the design and creation of motivational telemarketing and telesales environments. Please call me at (216)499-7920.

Final Words

The need for telephone environments to be motivating never has been in question. *Finding* new and different ways to create and maintain this stimulating atmosphere *is* the perplexing question facing you and I, and this will be an everlasting challenge. Contests represent a large piece to the puzzle, and this book will provide you with what you need to know to plan and execute them effectively.

So, welcome aboard, and thanks again for joining me on what I promise to be an interesting, fun, and profitable journey for you.

Your friend,

Dave Worman
Canton, Ohio
November, 1992

1. The "Motivational" Atmosphere

Failing to do it can — and does — cost managers their jobs.

It's a hot topic at telemarketing conventions, as managers congregate at break-out sessions and in the hallways as they quiz each other, "How do YOU do it?"

I'm talking about motivating your telephone professionals.

But what is motivation, really?

According to Webster, motivation is "something from within that prompts or incites an action; an inner drive, impulse or intention that causes a person to do something or act in a certain way."

And much of the conventional wisdom out there says the only way to get a person to do something is to make them want to do it. My experience (which sometimes has been painful) causes me to make three additions to that thought:

The *BEST* way to get a person to do something *WELL* is to *HELP* them *WANT* to do it.

In general, there seems to be two theories to motivation. Some emphatically believe it is possible to have motivational influence on your personnel or literally motivate people which is known as "external driven motivation."

Perhaps you have experienced a situation where one of your managers tried to motivate you. Ever had goals thrust upon you by a well-intentioned superior . . . . goals that maybe were more disheartening than motivating? Many of us have.

On the other hand, hopefully you've been in situations where the environment was conducive to you motivating yourself. Believers, including me, of this "internal driven motivation" are convinced that motivation must come from within the person, and that management is responsible for creating the positive conditions which stimulate self-motivation. How to create that atmosphere within your telemarketing environment will always be one of the most critical roles for management.

To maintain an atmosphere that encourages self motivation is the ultimate challenge and remains a mystery for many telesales, telemarketing, customer service, and other call center supervisors, managers, and even senior level executives. To begin solving this mystery let's look at creating and maintaining the positive atmosphere necessary for self-motivation.

How to Create a Climate that is Self-Motivating

This book, indeed, is about sales contests. That's why you bought it. However, they can't be run — effectively — in a vacuum. It'd be like buying a book on exercising so you could lose weight, while at the same time not addressing eating habits that included a steady diet of pizzas, oreos, french fries, candy, and ice cream. Other elements need to be in place to make sure you show success.

To make contests work, several things need to be in place. I'm going to just touch briefly on them in this chapter . . . . starting right now.

The Solid Compensation Plan

Compensation still remains atop the employee list of motivational factors for telephone professionals. Because of this, a solid pay structure is the foundation for creating and maintaining a positive work environment. It is imperative that your reps feel appreciated when it comes to their overall compensation.

Your people should feel that the company wants them to succeed and know that when they do they will receive a piece of the "pie."

Wages, commissions, and bonuses will vary depending on the telephone function being performed. Outbound sales typically will earn more than the inbound; corporate positions usually more than service agencies; a business-to-business pay structure will normally be higher than business-to-consumer; business-to-business reps often get a base salary while business-to-consumer are paid hourly, and the list goes on. Your pay structure should be focused on the job description.

For instance, my current staff is divided into three different job responsibilities and the pay structure reflects this. My service account specialists are salaried higher than the telemarketing sales associates . . . . who are in turn salaried higher than the telemarketing research representatives. This "step ladder" effect acts as a stimulant because there is opportunity for growth within the department.

Also, make sure that your reps' base pay (salary or hourly) is equal to or above the market standard. If it is not, you could subject your company to losing good employees for two reasons: they will go where the money is, and, secondly, they will leave because they feel unappreciated. If you are trying to build an atmosphere that stimulates self-motivation, an unstable compensation plan *is not* the way to get started.

Paying Commissions and Bonuses are Musts
Commissions and bonuses should be a part of every telemarketing or telesales compensation plan. Once you have a established your objective incite your people to exceed those goals. The most successful plans reward the high achievers and weed out the under achievers. And contrary to some belief, commissions and bonuses do not always need to be *cash*. In fact, I have found through experimenting that there are other ideas which will work better than cash in some cases. My staff is currently commissioned on a monthly basis with option for additional bonuses every quarter. Instead of cash, I work with the Olsen O'Leary (Pittsburg, PA) catalog company. My reps earn points which translate into dollars to be spent exclusively within the catalog that features gifts, including appliances, clothing, household items, jewelry and even fabulous trips. They are more turned on by this catalog than

cash because they say "cash would just go into my gas tank or to the grocery store." This way they can—and do— look at their catalog week in and week out, fantasizing about what they want to "buy" for themselves or family members. Some choose to spend by the quarter; others build it up for the entire year.

Haven't we all looked through catalogs mentally choosing things we couldn't afford? If you are like me, the answer is yes! This catalog concept makes dreams come true. My reps have been able to purchase televisions, cam corders, his/hers bicycles, other extravagant gifts and in a few cases, fabulous trips . . . . things they wouldn't normally have the money to enjoy. It also becomes a natural for contests by rewarding your people in points instead of cash in many cases.

Regardless of type or amount, I recommend commissions be issued on a monthly basis and bonuses every quarter. If stretched out much longer your employees will lose sight of the "light at the end of the tunnel." Commission and bonus days are exciting for your reps and a perfect time for managers to recognize the achievements that earned those bonuses. Your plan will never be perfect . . . . and consequently needs to be reviewed periodically and refined if necessary.

Employee Recognition

How often do you recognize your employees for their accomplishments? I think if each of us took a structured test with questions based on this, we would all have the same outcome: NOT ENOUGH.

Accomplishments are achievement.

We all starve for recognition. It's like a present. We all love presents no matter what size, shape or color.

Recognition can be given in so many different ways. I think most of us don't get enough . . . . so we don't give enough.

Think for a minute about the recognition you would like to receive more of. Think of the last time your boss said "Great job." (Hopefully it wasn't that long ago, but sadly, for many it is.) How did you feel? When was the last time you received *written* recognition for an accomplishment? Didn't you show it to people at work and at home? And then what? I am sure it is either hanging up conveniently within sight or filed somewhere where it will be safe. Recognition is appreciation, and don't we all like to be appreciated? This form of positive reinforcement is the spark needed to rekindle every TSR's fire, and you should make sure the fire continues to burn.

The Price is Right: FREE
The greatest advantage of recognition is price. Most of it is free, and your return is monumental. It is the best investment you can make. If banks could only give us the same return on investment from our savings accounts!

There isn't a day that goes by that I do not tell those that deserve it "Thanks for a great day," or "I appreciate the effort. Thanks." They are sent home after a long day with an upper that will spill over to the next day and beyond. I leave similar messages on voice mail to individuals . . . . or everyone on special occasions.

Written recognition is equally important. "Little things mean a lot" becomes an understatement regarding recognizing your people. One issue I would caution you on that can have detrimental results is recognizing equally—or over recognizing—the undeserving. When you are guilty of this you diminish the value of your appreciation to the ones who truly deserve it. If those who have not earned recognition receive it equally, it's cheapened in the minds of those who are entitled to it.

Only those that *achieve* should *receive,* and in front of their peers. I make it a practice to recognize individual accomplishments within range of others' ears. I'll also pin up special recognition on the department bulletin board for all eyes to see. Treat a star performer to lunch with upper-management. When you have visitors, let an achiever have the honor of giving the department tour.

Here are some other examples of non-monetary motivation that I have used to recognize my people for hard work and achievement:

- Give a special parking space to the employee who "drives" the hardest.

- A California Raisin to person who has the highest percentage of "raisin" their productivity from the previous week/month.

- Hang cardboard stars in the TSR's area for any "star studded" performance.

- Poster size playing cards: King or Queen of the week based on calling goals. All four aces together to tell someone they're "all aces."

- Place a large replica of phonograph record in the area of anyone setting a "record" for calls, completes, sales, etc.

- Plaques or trophies for special accomplishments or achievements.

These are only examples. I also have "negative" rewards that create positive stimulation. A ketchup bottle for the person who needs to play "catch up" in their productivity or a toy dragon for those whose sales are "draggin." These create instant energy to improve . . . as no one wants either of these to be seen in their area for long. In fact, I have a seen my people go from the Dragon or Ketchup Bottle to the Raisin or Record within a very short period of time. If you're wondering where to get these non-monetary motivators, novelty stores have been my greatest resource. In most cases they are relatively inexpensive.

This important subject of recognition will be further explored in this chapter and in other chapters throughout the book.

Remember, think about what's on *your* wish list for recognition and use that as a guide for giving it to your employees . . . . whether you get it or not from your superiors.

Goals and Expectations

What you expect from your people needs to be established and shared with each employee.

This painting of the company picture should include both short-term and long-term individual goals, as well as an overall view of the company goals. Making sure that everyone is aware of the corporate goals is essential. But this will only set the stage. All of your performers must know their roles and how their individual achievements will impact the overall production.

Maybe this has happened to you: Your boss says at the beginning of a year, "We need a big year," or maybe, " . . . . looking for big things out of you this year." What constitutes "a big year"? What "big things" are you expected to achieve? And then, at the end of the year, you hear "Well we didn't have the big year that we wanted," or, "Why didn't you achieve those big things we expected of you?"

Cloudy goals and vague communication will leave employees uncertain of what is expected of them. Be specific about your expectations.

Goals are definitely a prerequisite to achievement. Here is a good example: There was a time when my annual goals for my department were not established until September 1 of that year. Before that point it was simply "make as many calls on as many projects as you can." Although performance was good and the atmosphere remained positive . . . . there was still something missing. Once I was aware of our department's expected productivity, I posted it for all to see: a giant poster board with a matrix of every remaining work day in that year and each employee's name accordingly. I met with my people, set the stage with corporate goals, confirmed personal roles, and sat back for the production.

What a difference from the first eight months of the year!

In those remaining four months my people increased their previous good performance by almost 40%. This rise in productivity was due only in part to clear expectations. Also, knowing what impact those achievements would have on the company made their goals more important to them, and, therefore, more achievable.

Even though corporate, division and department goals will help everyone drive as a team, individual goals are a necessity for your TSRs to focus on day-by-day calling activity. Too often, looking at annual corporate goals can be overwhelming unless you break them down by months, weeks, days and even hours. Time and time again I see companies that set merely annual goals only to have their employees perceive them to be unattainable by May or June. Even though they may still be achievable, your ship will sink if your crew feels there is no hope.

Meet with every employee and establish individual goals based on employee capabilities. The more you break the targets down — months, weeks, days, hours — the easier it will be for your people to know where they stand all the time. They will be more in-tune on a consistent basis.

My current staff knows how many calls-per-hour they should make on each project; the percentage of decision makers-to-contacts they should reach; how often they should convert contacts into leads; and all other pertinent formulas surrounding their day-to-day call activity. We also post corporate and department goals throughout our area helping each of them understand their contribution to the overall bottom line. People who know where they are going, (and who also know how to get there and what impact they will have) tend to out-perform those with little knowledge of company direction.

The purpose of goals is to focus your attention. Your mind will not reach toward achievement until it has clear objectives.

Remember the magic begins when we set goals. The switch is flipped, the current begins to flow, and the power to accomplish becomes a reality.

Training

Structured training for your telephone professionals is imperative. And, ongoing instruction and further education can be an effective tool in maintaining a positive atmosphere.

For instance, in 1990 and 1991 I made sure to take my people to at least one off-site work related seminar. Skills and techniques sometimes need to be emphasized by someone other than the manager. In 1992 I was able to budget a certain dollar amount for each representative to use for further education off-site. They are able to check with seminar services or my lists of appropriate opportunities and choose those that they feel will address their needs. The final decisions must then be based on my approval. Upon their return they are required to formally present the seminar's highlights to the rest of the team. This assures the reps' focused attention at the seminar, and your whole team benefits although only one person attends.

These group sessions act as an additional stimulant for the attendees . . . . giving them an opportunity to help educate their teammates.

This form of further education is very feasible for smaller staffs or large company budgets that can support medium size groups. When this is not possible due to large staff size, lack of budget dollars, or a combination of the two, a few on-site seminars during the course of the year can be very cost efficient. Too often companies fail to recognize the value of ongoing training and subsequently suffer later on.

It has been proven over and over that effective training builds self-confidence which enhances the productivity of employees. Higher performance levels in turn provide self motivation by the very fact that most people have a natural desire to succeed.

Remember you cannot possibly "overtrain" your telephone personnel.

On-Going Training is Essential

The tendency of many telemarketing representatives is to wrongly assume that once they have been initially trained they do not need refresher courses. Unfortunately, many managers add to this misconception by not developing further training programs.

Even the finest automobile in the world needs regular tune ups to maintain quality operation. After your initial training, implement periodical "tune-up appointments" for the following basics that will always need ongoing attention for maximum effectiveness:

- Communication: listening skills; telephone etiquette and techniques

- Product Knowledge

- Sales Skills

- Welcoming Objections

- Closing Techniques

- Probing Skills

- Customer Satisfaction

These appointments can sometimes be for individuals, teams or even for your whole group depending on the size of your staff. As Regional Telemarketing Manager for *USA Today*, I implemented the concept of team appointments by grouping portions of my staff together periodically for tune ups on general skills or very specific techniques. These sessions can include appropriate training materials, audio tapes, and even role playing with managers as the customer.

Be proactive with these regular tune-ups. Don't wait for a breakdown.

Monitoring and Coaching

A coaching program affiliated with call monitoring should also be a structured portion of the ongoing training.

All monitoring that identifies a need for coaching attention should result in immediate discussion between the TSR and supervisor or manager performing the monitoring. Time lapse here can create problems due to lack of memory on both parts. If you need to coach them regarding a particular issue or issues about a certain call, it must be done prior to the next call. Otherwise, the representative's mind becomes filled with additional call information and they are less likely to clearly remember the incidents you are trying to focus on. This will dramatically diminish the impact of your help. Anytime I identified a need during monitoring and did not address it promptly I usually heard the following remarks upon discussion with the representative: "I don't remember saying that," or "I don't think I said that," or even "Which call was that?" Ineffective? Totally.

The points you want to improve need to be fresh in their mind as well as yours.

Don't Forget to Give the Positive Feedback

Positive attention when monitoring needs equally quick reaction from management for the same reasons. Anything from exceptional introductions through closing a sale deserves immediate stroking.

Unlike improvement discussions which should always remain private, back-patting can and should often be done in front of co-workers. Hearing praise or compliments directed at others can often create a fifth gear in people that rarely surfaces otherwise. They will now push harder than ever to hopefully receive the same praise or compliments earlier given to one of their fellow-workers.

An evaluation form for monitoring should be used to document the results of all monitoring sessions and should be signed by both the manager or supervisor and the TSR following discussion. Monitoring and recoaching should be considered a no-lose activity by everyone in your environment when performed in a positive manner on a regular basis. When you share the positive results after monitoring, it creates a natural high. When recoaching is necessary you will be enhancing their subsequent productivity, therefore, providing a stimulant.

The initial expense for providing effective ongoing training may sometimes seem high, but when you consider the motivational impact it can have and the cost of employee turnover, it becomes a wise investment that will pay high dividends.

Solid Communication

Another vital element for a self-motivating environment is solid communication. The impact generated by sound communication between management and the employees plays an important role in creating and sustaining a positive climate. Here are some ideas:

● **As a manager, establish an open door policy at all times.** Let your people know you are there for them. When it comes to open door policies, my people know that my door is "off the hinges." They know this because I have always let them know "if something is important enough that you need me, it instantly becomes equally important to me because *I need you.*" And, I demonstrate that. When one of my employees needs a question answered, an idea considered, a paper signed, a sounding block, etc., they know I will stop what I am doing and turn my attention to them. They are my production, so whenever I am needed they know I'm there. Whether your door is open, closed and locked with blinds drawn shut, or whether you have a private office at all is irrelevant. When your people need you . . . . be there.

● **Involve your employees as much as possible in meetings pertaining to their function.** Schedule weekly or monthly team meetings and make sure you get input from all employees during that time. When having meetings regarding new or existing calling campaigns, I include the reps who are working on that project. Remember, they are on the front line closest to the situation and their input can be invaluable. Their feeling of importance also grows with additional involvement. For example, I involve my reps in meetings that discuss project objectives, scripting, and when needed, data summary. They have a better feel for the project when they understand the objective. I also find my reps to be a tremendous resource in scripting meetings. Where better to have input from regarding how something will flow or sound on the phone? For instance, when it comes time for data summarization for market research projects, their feedback regarding the completed surveys is critical. This also supplies them with satisfaction as to "What happens with all that great data we collected?" These are only a few examples. Don't leave your people out of the information loop regarding the project you want them to complete. My experience has been, the more they're involved, the better the project goes.

● **If possible, speak to your people briefly before each shift begins answering any questions and energizing them.** At *USA Today* I was physically able to start most shifts with five minutes of announcements including business such as script changes, contest rules or calling goals as well as anything the reps wanted to share personally as time permitted. This daily proactive pump seems to help people jump off to a positive start. My current position often does not allow me the luxury of energizing my team in person prior to work beginning. When I am unable to be there in person due to other responsibilities, there are other ways to perform this motivational liftoff. At times I will photocopy a motivational message, leaving a copy in each person's inbasket or on their desks. Like many companies in the 90's, our phone system includes voice mail which can be an effective tool when used to present preshift announcements along with positive encouragement.

● **An inhouse newsletter that carries personal-related stories as well as business-oriented news.** Along with other Diebold departments, Corporate Telemarketing is located in a downtown office tower. Recently a Tower Team was put together to design and publish a monthly newsletter now known as *"Tower Talk."* It includes updated corporate news but focuses on news surrounding the departments located specifically at the tower. There is always a feature article about a different department, restaurant coupons, crossword contests and success stories regarding peoples' personal lives. News about their children, extra curricular activities, special anniversaries, birthdays, etc. Everyone anxiously awaits the monthly arrival of *Tower Talk* as it generates laughter, excitement, and a lot of pride as we read about ourselves as well as the lives of other employees.

It's fun to watch the expression of pride as an individual reads about personal achievements and those of family members ... the excitement that's created when someone in your area wins one of the *Tower Talk* contests .... or even the teasing that takes place regarding a birthday or special anniversary.

Everyone likes to see their name in print associated with positive recognition .... and the restaurant coupons are great! It enhances the overall synergy between different positions, departments, and most of all, people.

● **Write letters or memos to your employees for special accomplishments.** This is an idea that is enormously effective but unfortunately underused. And that's sad because it's so easy to do! How much time does it take to type or even write down a few paragraphs? Not long at all. And what is the impact if you do? TREMENDOUS! These letters don't always have to be written by you. As my teams complete calling campaigns for different Diebold departments, I periodically receive appreciation letters from the project originator thanking me for a job well done. I don't ever file these without thanking my people with my own comments and signature with copies going to those who worked on the project. The rep ends up being recognized twice; once indirectly by the project originator, and next, most importantly, by me, their manager. These cost-free forms of motivation become proudly-displayed forms of stimulation in their personal work areas.

● **Similar letters should periodically come from senior-level management.** Executive recognition by letter will always succeed in boosting the ego of any employee. In our overall war of finding effective motivational methods, this secret weapon will help win many battles for you. However, the key to any secret weapon is the timing. And I caution you: overkill will result by using it too often. If I am initiating the action, I have always made sure that executive recognition is only affiliated with very special accomplishments. That way, because it is a rare occurrence, it escalates in motivational value. There are also times this will happen unexpectedly. For instance, in 1991, companies throughout the city of Canton, Ohio were asked by the local Junior Achievement Chapter for volunteers to help with the annual membership drive by telephone. Diebold responded by offering the services of their true telephone professionals: my staff. At the end of the five-day drive my people had produced 30% of their overall contributions. Not only did they receive a thank you letter from the Junior Achievement, they also got one from the president of Diebold congratulating them on their efforts.

What happened was that the same thank you letter sent from Junior Achievement was also sent to our president. He then recognized my staff's efforts in a letter of his own. The impact of these letters one after the other was phenomenal!

Make sure your senior-level management understands the importance of rewarding your people with recognition for significant achievements or special moments. These documented "Thank You's" will act as a remotivator every time they are read.

• **Verbally recognize your people with praise individually, or at times, as a team.** Once again a little of this goes a long way. I have always used preshift announcements, voice mail, and post shift briefings to verbally recognize my people individually and as a team. I also share individual accomplishments with everyone by praising that person in front of their teammates. Too often people hear only the bad news. Successful managers are those who recognize the importance of stressing the positive. The old saying "No news is good news" is just that: old, and outdated. The more I recognize my staff for a job well done, the harder they try to do it better. Coincidence? I don't think so. Writing and verbally passing positive energy will have a powerful effect on your employees.

• **Another component of good communication skills is one-on-one sessions with each employee to discuss outside interests as well as business issues.** Some of these should be scheduled, others spontaneous. I'm not talking about formal performance reviews. I try to have a one on one with each of my employees every quarter. Although business is the theme and we discuss current performance levels and goals, outside interests and personal news gets equal time. In addition to these scheduled events I will occasionally call employees into my office or I will visit them in their area to simply "check their pulse." Take some time to really know your people.

Bottom line, you'll get the best results when you genuinely *care about your people!* There is an old saying that states "People don't care how much you know until they know how much you care."

What REALLY Motivates Your People?

The real exploration in this journey to motivation becomes one of getting inside the minds of your people. Do you really know what motivates your employees? You must be able to answer "yes" to this question before you can successfully begin constructing this positive environment.

Studies show that in many cases what employers *think* motivates their people and what *actually* motivates their people are very far apart. The chart on the next page summarizes a recent study, presented at TelemarketPlace '91, comparing what employers feel motivates their telemarketing professionals and in reality what does motivate these same employees. The numbers are ranked in order based on importance.

This and other similar studies consistently show working conditions rated very high in terms of importance to people who perform their job over the telephone. Mangers often mistakenly limit these conditions to the comfort level of a desk and chair.

What Motivates Telephone Professionals?
(Ranked in Order of Importance)

What Employers Think		What Employees Say
1	Appreciation	4
2	Involvement/planning	7
3	Sympathy	10
4	Job Security	5
5	Wages	1
6	Interesting Work	3
7	Promotion	6
8	Employer Loyalty	8
9	Working Conditions	2
10	Tactful Discipline	9

The Atmosphere You Create is Important
What about a positive atmosphere?

Atmosphere is a critical part of working conditions and a *positive* atmosphere enhances performance and productivity. When making important decisions that will impact the atmosphere within your telemarketing environment always look in a mirror and think about how well the idea would stimulate *you*. If it fails at this point, chances are very good it will not succeed with your personnel and it is time to look at alternative ideas.

Learn what motivates your people and exploit it. People will be motivated by different means. Although some things will effectively stimulate everyone, you must find the "key" that unlocks the door to each person's motivational world. Once inside, use that knowledge to set up your motivation game plan that will reach everyone. Flexibility is essential here. Some need a daily pat on the back while others need extra listening attention; some are incited by cash, others by prizes. Some take "time off" rewards at the end of a day, others prefer the morning.

Watching your peoples' reactions in different circumstances will help you identify their key to motivation. But, the very best way to uncover their secret is very simple: Ask them.

People will act on *their* motives, not yours. One of the clues to solving the mystery of maintaining a positive atmosphere in telemarketing environments is finding creative ways to push the ever changing motivational buttons of your employees. Peoples' motives, emotions and priorities are constantly changing . . . . and you must be prepared to inject fresh and exciting ideas into the motivational bloodstream of your telephone professionals.

One of the Best Answers: Contests

One way of successfully maintaining positive working conditions in telephone environments is utilizing **contests** to stimulate your people.

Think about it. When is the last time you saw someone — anyone — who didn't want to win?

Everyone has that built-in desire to succeed in a competitive atmosphere. But, only properly designed, implemented, and supervised contests will help sustain a positive, productive work environment. In an industry where burnout is a problem waiting to happen, and turnover can be very high, it becomes imperative to develop fun methods of maintaining and even enhancing employee performance levels.

Contests can have such a stimulating effect on employees, yet they are not utilized nearly enough in telemarketing environments.

Why? That's the question I asked myself when I was hired by *USA Today* in 1986 as Assistant Telemarketing Manager. One of my first observations of our center was the increase in productivity during any competitive contest.

Knowing that performance levels will naturally escalate during any competition, my question became . . . . "What would happen if we add fun to the competition?" In retrospect I might have just asked, "What happens when you light a stick of dynamite?"

An *EXPLOSION*, that's what!

Our sales went through the roof! The more contests I created, the higher our sales volume soared. There's no secret formula. The *fun* is the necessary spark that will light the motivational fire of your TSR's.

Regardless of whether you are inbound or outbound, business-to-consumer, or business-to-business, it is irrelevant to the success of creating contests.

So, if all this is so obvious, the question is still . . . . why? *Why* are contests so underused in telemarketing environments across the world? Insufficient time and creativity usually seem to be the missing ingredients when contests are underused.

Managers need to make the time to be creative.

Too busy and not a creative bone in your body, you say? Don't fear. You are about to embark upon a reading journey that will answer your contest questions along the way. We'll cover:

- Why do contests work?

- What contests work best?

- When should you run them and how often?

- What are some prize ideas?

- What should be the call goals during a contest?

- How do we deal with post-contest blues?

And, best of all, we are going to provide you with step-by-step examples of contests you can adapt and use in your own departments.

One element you're on you own with, though, is enthusiasm. Ralph Waldo Emerson once said, "Nothing great was ever accomplished without enthusiasm."

You'll need to create the initial feelings of enthusiasm and then use contests to create an epidemic of enthusiasm in your telemarketing environment. It will become contagious. And as it spreads, turnover will go down and performance will go up.

2. Why Do Contests Work?

Could a chapter consist of only one word?

This one could: Competition.

When you think about why contests are successful in telephone environments, *competition* is your number one answer.

And, don't you love it when you hear people analyzing others (with a critical tone) by saying things like "They're very competitive," or "He/she is too competitive," and similar such remarks.

Who's kidding who here?!

It's part of our human nature to be competitive. Like it or not, it is part of the package that we're all born with. However, it does come in many different sizes.

Think for a moment of your own competitive spirit .... when did you first notice it? Do you enjoy competition? What situations stimulate your competitive juices most?

I can recall being very competitive at a very early age. If you grew up with brothers or sisters you know what I mean. Remember competing for parental attention? Or to be better in academics or sports? To be better at anything .... everything?

I'm sure you're thinking back either with a sly smile or a sneer. And, oh, how parents will exploit this competitive need.

I can still see my mom reeling us kids in, hook, line and sinker!

The house I grew up in has a mammoth buckeye tree on the property. Although shiny buckeyes have a certain beauty to them, they make a terrible mess in the yard when they fall by the hundreds. My mom used to stimulate the competitive spirit in my brothers and I; I can still hear her saying to the three of us, "I want you to pick up all the buckeyes in the yard and (here was the catch) let's see who can pick up the most."

It didn't matter if she offered a reward or prize. Oh, sure, she sometimes dangled an incentive in front of us; sometimes it was a whole shiny quarter. Other times it was the choice of a favorite upcoming dinner.

But to us . . . . it didn't matter! Prize or no prize, it was enough for each brother to try and pick up more buckeyes than the other two. To compete, to win . . . . that was the ultimate conquest.

Bring back any memories? Probably not specifically with buckeyes, but perhaps your parents were equally or more creative at times.

And aren't we supposed to learn from our parents? Did you? I did!

You should see my three kids scramble when I put up a quarter to see which one can find the lost bone that our golden retriever (Dusty) left or conveniently hid somewhere. And to my eldest daughter Michelle, the quarter is totally insignificant. The competition of finding the bone before Jackie or Danny is the driving force.

And believe me, that same driving force is very alive in your TSR's. A portion of it will surface naturally, especially in working environments where people are performing the same function. It is normal for a certain amount of peer competition to be evident. People naturally want to outperform each other for two reasons: Number one, we're all somewhat selfishly inclined. There is a certain gratification in knowing that you outperformed your co-workers. And number two is the desire—that lies in most of us—to be the best employee in the eyes of management. As always, some people possess a higher level of intensity here, but, the basic desire resides inside all of us. And a natural surge in competitive spirit will occur during organized contests.

Why this takes place is simple: the spotlights are shining. Everyone is on center stage. This naturally produces additional adrenalin in most people.

Recognizing Accomplishments Gets Excitement

In Chapter 1, I stressed the importance of recognizing your employees. This critically important factor will be reemphasized throughout the book. Recognition plays a major role in why contests are effective in telephone environments.

Remember, most people starve for recognition; contests provide a golden opportunity for them to get recognized for their achievements.

The more they achieve the more they get recognized.

That additional recognition doesn't normally take place during the course of everyday activities. At least it doesn't happen as often as it should.

When a contest is announced, your people can *taste* the opportunity for that additional recognition, and, consequently, are stimulated to produce more.

In a previous career I was Public Relations Manager for players on the Cincinnati Bengals football team, and had the opportunity to observe what motivated these sports stars. Even at the professional athletic level – even though we are talking about larger dollars and bigger egos – the bottom line is . . . . competition!

I'm sure there will be some contention here that pro sports is just big business and that the players only care about the dollars involved. Nonsense! These thoughts are predominantly driven by media exploitation of only a portion of these athletes who do rest

on their laurels and don't give 100% all of the time (or even most
of the time) and those who think they should get paid even more.

But the key word here is *portion*. Only a small sample of these
athletes share this attitude.

The world of professional athletics is no different than the regular
world of business. Don't you have those same individuals that
want to get paid more or that don't work as hard as they should,
or as often as they should?

Sure you do. I do too. So does every business that employs
people. But, I've also seen the other side of the coin up close.

The intensity of competition to win roster spots in training camp;
the ongoing fight for playing time week in and week out; the
kicked-in locker when someone else is chosen to start; the anger
at reporters, or a helmet smashed into pieces following a loss.
(No, not a playoff loss.... *a preseason loss.*) The tears after defeat,
and victory as well. Is all of this about money or prizes?

Don't be grossly mistaken!

These emotions are internally driven by competitive spirit. The
need to win. The desire to be the best. The pain or humiliation
of not performing well. To borrow a phrase, the thrill of victory
and agony of defeat.

I've seen as much emotional intensity following an interteam
scrimmage at training camp as I have in the locker room following
the Super Bowl.

Is it fair comparing the competition in pro football with what takes
place in our telemarketing centers?

Absolutely! Remember, we're looking at what's inside people
regardless of their occupation. That internal flame flickers within
us all . . . . and begs to be stoked.

I contend that most people will fight as hard to earn a candy bar as they will a $25 check. I've seen it happen. I continue to see it happen. And, *I make it happen.*

Non-monetary Methods of Recognition
In Chapter 1, I shared some of the non-monetary motivation items I've used in my telephone environments, past and present. They represent a perfect example of this theory.

Take the California Raisin. When this little item goes up for grabs (to the person who has the highest percent of "raisin" their productivity) it creates as much energy in the room as any contest I've ever created. Everyone wants the prestige of mounting this $1.00 toy as a trophy in their area.

Egos? You bet! They know it's a status symbol.

The same thing happens with my little Oscar for Top Producer or Pillsbury Doughboy for the TSR "raisin the most dough."

It's the fun of competing against co-workers for recognition.

Recognition Works With Teams Too
The same result is produced with team concept contests.

Whenever I institute a team concept contest where everyone works to reach a group goal, the competitive intensity is equally as visible as it is in individual situations. The only difference is the fact that they are working as a team competing against a number or the clock, or in some cases, both.

Again, in many cases the prize is somewhat insignificant. Once you have appealed to people's motivation with a challenge, they will attack that challenge with escalated effort.

One of the best things about group goals is listening to the people verbally supporting each other as they work toward reaching the designated goal as a team.

The enthusiastic intensity becomes contagious and spreads like a forest fire during a drought.

In fact, whenever I implement a contest with a team goal as the theme, one of the TSR's will always step forward and take the lead role; of being the cheerleader to a certain extent . . . . periodically going around to his or her teammates checking on totals, encouraging effort, and backpatting accomplishment while still performing his or her own phone work in conjunction with the goal.

Self imposed peer pressure becomes very real in these situations as no one wants to feel like they are letting down the team. Word spreads quickly around the room as to how everyone is doing; the pressure is always on to carry your end of the load.

Many times team or group oriented contests may have better results based on that very fact. No one wants to bear the cross of being labeled as the one who didn't contribute . . . . especially if the goal is not met and the ultimate prize is not awarded.

Often I have put together team oriented contests to let everyone leave work early on a particular day if certain goals are reached. Usually even the lowest performing TSR's produce effectively during these contests, stimulated by the fear of standing out as the weak link.

It is easy at times to go virtually unnoticed in a contest that rewards individuals for reaching certain performance goals first or most. But not when you are being counted on by others to contribute a certain amount in order for the entire team to win.

If you played little league baseball, you're familiar with this same type of feeling. Picture one of those games where all your team-mates had a hit or perhaps made a good play in the field . . . . and you went 0 for 4 with one error in the field. That feeling of embarrassment, loneliness, and even depression would set in.

But, wouldn't additional drive and desire also set in? It sure did with me and I'll bet the same is true for most of you as well. That concentration and burning desire to get a hit and contribute sure took control of me in those cases.

Compete With Other Offices In Your Company

Those of you with multiple locations have a terrific opportunity for what I call "interleague play." Office against office. The employees of the winning office might receive a candy bar from the employees of the losing office. Or a can of pop.

Big prizes are not necessary here. Just competition.

At *USA Today* we often went office against office in sales-related contests. I would contact one of the other Regional Managers or vice versa and we would quickly put together numbers and decide on a contest theme and a prize.

Did this stimulate the competitive juices of our TSR's? Are you kidding? We are talking about company bragging rights here!

I strongly recommend this interleague competition for those of you with multiple locations.

Activity is Essential for Contest Success

Beyond competition, another contributing factor in why contests are effective in telemarketing environments is the activity associated with the contest itself.

All of us in this world of business by phone are well aware of the rapid burnout level caused primarily by the redundancy of call after call after call. Having a contest is one thing. However, if you want your success ratio to improve, attach physical activity to as many of your contests as possible.

It's amazing how stimulating it can be for TSR's to simply get up out of their chair a few times a shift to engage in contest-related activity.

If you've personally spent time on the phone you know what I mean. Think back briefly and it will come to you quickly I'm sure.

I know myself nothing was as rejuvenating as getting away from the phone . . . . if only for a few brief moments. To do so was stimulating in itself, but to engage in some *fun activity* related to competition is icing on the cake.

And in case you are thinking "I don't want my reps out of their chairs, I want them dialing more numbers," let's dig deeper into that issue.

Everyone who has a job that requires long periods of time sitting down enjoys getting out of their chair, stretching and moving around. To the coffee machine, the restroom, anywhere. It's a break from repetition, both mentally and physically.

A Physical and Emotional Break
Your body needs it, because the way you feel physcially drives the way you think.

It's no secret that positions in telemarketing lend themselves to a great deal of repetition, and at times, monotony. More than most people in other professions, people in our industry need to be able to periodically get up from their station and briefly move about. And they need to know that it's OK to do that. Repetition is part of this job; monotony need not be.

According to Webster, monotonous is defined as "dull and wearisome." Should your TSR's look at their job as *dull and wearisome?* If they do, what kind of performance can you expect? The answer is the kind that is driven by dull and wearisome attitudes.

You can avoid monotony by not gluing your people to their chairs. In fact, in my environments both past and present, performance seems to be at its best when people are occasionally taking a stretch from the phone. I encourage this all of the time — contest or no contest.

Don't misunderstand, though. I'm not suggesting 15-minute breaks here; those should already be built into your shifts. I'm referring to very brief moments. And when TSR's are aware that performance will earn them the right to get out of their chairs three or four extra times a shift, they will push extra hard.

Part of the push comes because of the status attached to contest activity in front of co-workers. You see, if you get up from your chair to perform any kind of activity related to a contest, that means you've reached the goals set before you. Your success is visible to your peers and your managers.

Stimulating? Every time.

A bonus is that it's equally stimulating to the rest of the people who now want to be in the spotlight engaging in whatever action is tied to the contest. I call this contest-related activity that takes place in front of co-workers "Action Attention."

Most people are naturally stimulated by showing off in front of others. And that's exactly what this is.

By reaching goals that management sets for a contest, a TSR has achieved the success and now gets to showcase that fact in front of an audience: your other reps.

Some contests may not lend themselves to related activity, but most will or should. You may need to be thinking about potential Action Attention as you create contests. Although it's not mandatory for success, I have found that it always increases your chances of being ultimately successful with any contest.

During my first year at *USA Today*, I put together a contest based on the popular TV game show Wheel of Fortune. The concept was good, and certainly the timing was excellent. The show was at the height of it popularity in the mid to late 1980's and just the mention of "big money" created enthusiasm.

When designing the contest I made one big mistake. Fortunately, I identified and corrected it after running **The Wheel** only two times.

I brought in a very small replica of the wheel from a board game at home. As my TSR's reached certain productivity goals to earn a spin of the wheel, one of my supervisors or I would take the tiny wheel to their station allowing them to spin for big money. Although there was excitement during the game, and it was moderately successful . . . . I could tell something was missing.

Can you can guess the mistake I made?

By taking this very small **Wheel of Fortune** to the people to let them spin it, I was cheating the audience as well as the contestant. Only that person and a few people around them ever knew what was going on. In fact, as people filed out at break time, I could hear them ask each other "Did you win anything" or "Did you get to spin the wheel yet?"

That's when I knew we were not maximizing enthusiasm. And at that point the solution came to me rather suddenly:

Everyone should know *who* has had a chance to spin the wheel, *who* has won, and *how much.*

I then made a huge wheel out of poster board, construction paper and a wood spinner, and put it up in the most conspicuous place in the center of the office. I put up poster boards with everyone's name in a matrix to follow the results from spinning the wheel.

As TSR's reached their goals, they now got out of their seat, went over to the wheel, and gave it a spin in front of the "studio audience."

When it stopped they got to mark the result of the spin beside their name.

All this in front of co-workers and managers as well. Action Attention. The ultimate stimulant.

Even the simplest forms of Action Attention are effective. Many times, past and present, I will simply divide the room into two or more groups and announce performance goals.

At a visible spot in the department will be poster boards matching the number of teams. As sales are made, each TSR goes up with a magic marker and changes the number of sales on his/her own team board and returns to his or her chair.

Now is this too much time away from the phone? Hardly. Is it too complicated? No. Is it effective? YES! And how simple can you get?

Once again proving that for the most part, the *prize* is not the number one issue. And the activity itself can often be relatively insignificant as well. What really matters is the pride of succeeding in front of others.

I have talked to hundreds of TSR's over the years and found that in general, the activity and potential prizes are actually less stimulating than the visibility and silent recognition that comes with Action Attention.

Throughout the book I will periodically reemphasize the need for this contest-related activity and give specific examples along the way. As you decide on what contests from Chapter 8 to use and when you are creating your own, make sure you ask yourself "What activity can I affiliate with this contest?"

Implement your answer, have some fun and then sit back for some positive results.

3. Which Contests Work Best?

Which contests *do* work best? Some would say that's the $64,000.00 question. Not me. Among telemarketing managers across North America this is becoming the *$64 MILLION question!*

And, there is no simple answer. In fact, the question "Which contests work best?" seems to drive supporting questions such as:

- Inbound or outbound?

- Does the age of employees make a difference?

- Are business-to-business environments different from business-to-consumer when it comes to contests?

- Are long or short contests better?

- Are large budgets necessary?

In this chapter we will find some answers to these questions — and more — while we discover what ingredients are necessary to develop successful contests.

Simple is Better

While there is no single solution to which contests work best, *creativity* and *variation* are the two most essential elements in designing contests that will work. When your "creative juices" flow, remember, *simple is better.* Contrary to popular belief, contest creativity is not limited to highly sophisticated ideas. Too often a great idea is wasted because it gets dragged out by a management philosophy that adds too many components to the rules, goals, and even prizes.

Let your imagination wander for a moment. Take a journey with me. Close your eyes for just a moment and when you reopen them to read the next paragraph you will be a Telephone Sales Representative . . . . . ready? *Go!*

> Management has just come up with a contest idea for your shift and as you listen to the rules and goals you become confused enough to ask the TSR next to you, "What combination of calls and sales do we need to win? And do we earn time off that equals 7% of last week's connect time based on a four-day work week? And did she say that if our call-per-hour ratio was lower than 35, we only earn 3% of the 7% possible, even if we reach the combined goal of total calls and sales? And then every credit card sale I get counts double after the second one? *Double what?!*
>
> Ten minutes later your head stops spinning and you spend another thirty minutes trying to figure out what you're supposed to do and what you will get if you do it.

Were you totally confused? Don't feel badly! That's exactly how the real TSR's felt when this contest was *actually* presented. That's right. True story!

As an assistant telemarketing manager at the time, I listened to that very conversation between TSR's and observed that most people were spending more time trying to piece together this hair-pulling puzzle than they were placing calls. Others weren't even trying to figure it out. They had thrown their hands up in the air in frustration. They simply didn't care.

And I spent the evening trying to intelligently explain something that *even I didn't understand.*

The mistake here is one I hope you learn from without having to pay the costly price like I did. The concept is good: if certain call goals are reached you will earn time off. But, this well-intentioned idea was turned into a disaster by cumbersome and unnecessary clauses and contingencies that the reps didn't comprehend — much less be motivated by.

However, even through my own frustration I saw a glimmer of potential in this contest. One week later, after some serious thought and number-crunching, I took the very same concept and made it work by simplifying the process. I hammered out all the success criteria in advance and announced to the TSR's "For every hour that you average 35 calls and one sale you will earn ten minutes of extra time off. After your second credit card sale, each credit card sale will be worth 20 minutes of free time."

This time there were no blank stares. Everyone understood clearly. They went to work, had some fun, and everyone won at least ten minutes of free time. By the way, the company won as well. Sales were up 15% over projection.

Excessive complexity will only make contests far too cumbersome for both you and your TSR's, and ultimately diminish the impact you want.

You Don't Have to Spend Much Either

Believing that large budgets are mandatory for successful contests is another common misconception among sales managers. This is the primary reason contests are not utilized as often as they should. The natural competitive spirit in most people makes budget issues almost insignificant. Not that contests with prizes such as elaborate trips or shopping sprees are not effective — they can be extremely motivating.

The key to remember is that lofty budget dollars and grand prizes are not a necessity for exciting and successful contests in your department. To prove this point let's look at a few very creative contests performed with minimal dollars that have been very successful.

"Control of the Roll"

The best example I know of was a contest created by Ken Van Vranken (Center Manager, MCI Services) while he was a telemarketing supervisor for a Chicago-based company in the early 1980s. This contest was actually designed around a *decreasing budget!* Things were so bad at this office that Ken was asked to squeeze the budget to get a space heater instead of repairing a broken furnace, and rationing all supplies . . . . even toilet paper (Ouch!). His people were dialing in gloves to stay warm. And all of this for *minimum wage.*

Despite the adverse conditions he had to work with, Ken still wanted to keep his people smiling. He created a positive situation out of potential negative disaster. He took the budget "squeeze" on toilet paper and created a contest called **Control of the Roll.** This contest was designed to incite his TSR's to make sales in order to have **Control of the Roll.** Once in control, you had the option to use the roll while in control, or chance that another TSR would make a sale and take over **Control of the Roll.**

When a sale was generated, the roll would be tossed like a football across the room to the new controller. This way everyone knew who had it. If you became "in need" of the roll, there were only two options: get a sale and take control, or, go up and *try* to borrow the roll from the controlling TSR. This option was obviously a bit uncomfortable. Picture yourself getting up, going across the room and stopping at the desk of the controller. Would you want all eyes and ears on you when you asked a teammate if you could borrow the toilet paper? Not me! Van Vranken remembers fondly, "This contest cost absolutely nothing but the time to create it. It was very popular and was a daily activity for a long time."

The "Money Hat" Contest
The next two examples are contests I developed years ago that are very simple, and again, inexpensive and easy to implement and supervise.

The first one is called **The Money Hat.** Purchase a styrofoam derby (local party goods store or novelty outlet) and a tabletop call bell. Tape dollar bills on the hat using Monopoly money or other simulated currency. Management then predetermines calling goals which are announced to the people, and numerous bell ringing times which are left undisclosed. When the shift begins, the first TSR to make a sale, appointment, lead, etc. gets the prestige of wearing **The Money Hat.** The hat then constantly is transferred from head to head as predetermined call goals are met by different TSR's. Management rings the bell at each of the undisclosed, preset times. Whoever has **The Money Hat** on when the bell rings wins cash. Fifteen rings a shift could be worth $1.00 each, or five rings at $3.00 each, or even three rings at $5.00 each. Associate fewer rings with higher rewards and scale your payoff accordingly.

Does it work? Among many others, Jeanette Fannin, Director of Sales and Marketing for Hardware Sales Company in Cordova, Tennessee says, "Yes!" and adds,

> "I took this idea back from one of Dave's presentations at a national telemarketing conference. The only difference is we use a horn instead of a bell. **The Money Hat** is an easy and inexpensive contest that generated rather quick high sales, enthusiasm and a lot of smiles. Ultimately, those smiles are passed on to our customers."

Pennie Barclay and Louise El-Murr, two of Jeanette's TSR's agree:

> "This contest is most unique and generates a lot of fun and excitement for us. Since the game is based on luck, anyone could be in possession of the hat when the horn is blown. You never know when you will be the lucky one!"

The Money Hat is certainly a positive motivator and a neat way to break up the monotony sometimes associated with continuous telephone sales.

"The Who, What, Or Where Poster Board"
I developed this next contest specifically around Halloween in 1987. The initial idea was to cover a poster of a famous person with self-sticking notes which acted as a costume by masking the person's identity. As my TSR's got sales that evening, they would go up and pull off a note removing part of the Halloween mask. When someone could finally identify the personality, they won a small trick-or-treat bag full of candy. But, they had to get a sale and pull off a note to earn the opportunity to guess the identity. I had three posters that night and went through all three of them!

As I watched buzz of activity heighten throughout the evening (along with the results), I realized this was a contest that could be used anytime with great results.

Here are the slightly expanded rules for the **Who, What, Or Where Poster Board**:

Purchase a poster of a celebrity, famous place or an object, and cover it with straight lines of very small self-sticking notes. Then put the poster board up in the most visible part of your center. Establish calling goals and announce them to your TSRs the day of the contest. As TSR's reach your goals, they can go up and pull off a note to reveal a small portion of the poster. This will continue until someone thinks they can identify "who, what, or where" the poster is. If the TSR is correct, a prize of your determination and the poster are awarded to that TSR. If incorrect, the contest continues until the poster is successfully identified. Depending on the size of your staff or the size of the poster, this contest can last up to seven days.

Here are some tips to enhance the **Who, What, Or Where Poster Board Contest.**

- A TSR must have a certain amount of self-sticking notes to make a guess. (Log each person's pulls.)

- Associate 25 to 40 percent of the notes with smaller awards, such as time off, extra breaks, cash, extra pulls and others.

- Write numbers on the back of the 25 to 40 percent of the notes and keep a master list of the awards those numbers represent.

- Use large posters and do not always cover them right side up (turn sideways or upside-down prior to covering with self-sticking notes).

I continue to use **The Money Hat** and the **Who, What, or Where Poster Board** on a regular basis and they remain enormously popular and highly effective. You can usually count on a 25-30% increase in productivity when using either of these.

Variety of Contests is Essential

Regardless of what contests you run, and how much you spend, it's critical that your contest ideas don't become stale.

As a manager or supervisor you must make it a priority to find the time for creative thinking. At times you may feel like you have exhausted your own creative resources. If this happens, have a contest to receive contest ideas from your employees. Whenever I do this I always receive ideas that I'm able to use. In addition to getting the benefit of a contest that works, you have a motivated employee who takes pride in knowing you used his/her idea.

But there's more! This idea helps me identify creative people within my department.

I think you'll agree that as we look to internally promote TSR's to group leaders or supervisors, creativity should be one of the characteristics we look for in people. It sure is with me!

While I was managing one of *USA TODAY'S* regional telemarketing offices, I promoted one of the best TSR's I ever had to supervisor partially based on his creativity among other positive attributes. Whenever I went out to my people for contest ideas, Frank Feldhaus always submitted a great idea.

Frank is now a manager at that very same *USA TODAY* regional office and you will have the luxury of enjoying some of his contest ideas later on in Chapter 8.

Your staff can be an unlimited source of ideas if you give them the chance; they know what motivates them. And, you might uncover your next supervisor!

Use Different Themes to Vary Your Contests

One suggestion to keep your contests fresh is to affiliate them with different themes, such as holidays, anniversaries, sports and culture. This will help reach the diverse interest levels of all your TSR's.

Holidays are a great opportunity for designing contests. Don't we all at least mentally recognize all holidays? Sure we do! That by itself makes these special days a natural target for contests. In addition, one of the most important elements for a successful contest will already be in place: the proper atmosphere. I highly recommend appropriate decorations around the office weeks in advance of upcoming holidays. Again, we're not talking about major budget dollars here. Actually, very inexpensive one-time purchases can be used every year for each holiday. I also let different groups of people put up the decorations.

Because your people are mentally aware of the significance of all holidays, it is very easy to get them further pumped up with a contest at that time. Especially some of the most popular ones such as Christmas, Easter, Thanksgiving, Valentine's Day, July 4th and Halloween.

Because actual calling activity can't take place on many of these days, make sure your contest happens *prior* to that day rather than after. I made the mistake — once — of having a contest after the fact.

Valentine's Day fell on a Sunday and I set up the contest for Monday instead of when it should have been: Friday. The anticipation of the holiday was long gone by Monday. There just wasn't the normal excitement in the air, and, consequently, the calling numbers validated that.

You need to set the tone in advance and have your contest when the holiday mood is at its peak: *on that day or just before.*

What About the "Minor" Holidays?

Whenever I'm at seminars and conferences presenting this subject of motivation by using contests, I'm always asked "What about the holidays that don't get as much attention? Are these also a good time for contests?"

My answer is always the same: Absolutely!

In fact, here is a perfect example:

I developed **Pot-O-Gold** a few years ago for St. Patrick's Day. It has turned out to be one of the favorites every year for TSR's and management. I usually see one of the highest increases in productivity during this contest. Be sure to put this on your "To do" list for March. Here are the rules:

- All TSR's and management have a casual dress day and wear something green.

- For reaching predetermined goals (each sale, appointment, lead, etc.), a TSR gets a green shamrock. (Purchased, or cut from green construction paper.) Bonus shamrocks are awarded for any orders with holiday-related criteria. This includes addresses/names/phone numbers that include Pat, Patrick, Saint, gold, 3/17, green, etc. and so on.

- At the end of the shift all shamrocks are placed in a hat for the lucky drawing.

- Three winners each receive a **Pot-O-Gold** (small black pot with $17.00 worth of quarters, dimes, nickels, pennies). Three winners represent March (3rd month), and $17 represents 17th day.

Have fun next March! You will find more great contest ideas for holidays in Chapter 8.

Celebrate Aniversaries

Although not as feasable as holidays, some famous anniversary dates will work when creating contests. Many of the same elements necessary for holiday contests are also important when using an anniversary as a theme.

You will need more effort to create the needed atmosphere as anniversaries for the most part are not as visible as holidays.

Similar to holiday contests, begin to set the mood weeks in advance with pictures and or signs and verbally plant the seed by sharing the significance of the anniversary you are using with your people.

Timing is again important, but unlike some holidays, chances are very good that you will be able to call on the exact date eliminating the concern of "before or after."

The best example I can give you of an anniversary idea is a contest I designed in 1987 based on the famous moonwalk by Neil Armstrong in July of 1969. I use this annually and it has become a real favorite. Here's how **Journey to the Moon** works:

- Break your TSR's into teams of "astronauts."

- Reaching calling goals (sales, appointments, leads, etc.) equals "fuel," which moves the team's craft into positions to land on the moon.

- Bonus "fuel" is awarded for any orders with anniversary-related criteria. This includes addresses/names/phone numbers that include Neil, walk, moon, 7/20, 1969, space, or Armstrong.

- Malfunctions caused by incorrectly filled out orders, incomplete phone presentations, etc., will delay safe landing. Additional sales, appointments and leads are needed to land.

- The first (or any) team of astronauts to land safely wins and receives awards. Astronauts providing the most fuel for each team mate moon walk receives an additional prize.

Sports Offer Unlimited Opportunities
Sports probably offer the widest variety of possibilities for different contest ideas.

Being the sports fanatic that I am, I have designed contests over the years affiliated with football, baseball, basketball and golf.

The best part about sports-related contests is that some of your rules and call goals can be interchangeable with different sports. For instance, your call goals that equal a touchdown in one contest might be the same for a home run in another. Many of your concepts can be the same but simply applied to different sports.

Another factor that makes sports contests so successful is the physical activity that I suggest be attached to them.

Whenever possible, design a contest that allows your TSR's to get out of their chairs for brief moments to engage in activity associated with the contest theme.

For instance, whenever I implement my basketball contest I bring in my Little Tikes basketball set, and as TSR's reach goals they get up from their chair and shoot real baskets trying to score for themselves or their team.

Another good example involves golf. Go out and purchase an inexpensive putt return device that pops the ball back to you whenever you make a putt. Then design your **"TGA Event"** (Telemarketing Golf Association). When your TSR's reach your predetermined goals, allow them to walk up the fairway to the green and putt in front of all the other spectators in the "gallery.

These types of authentic activities can be very stimulating and when supervised properly, will not be disruptive to your environment.

Remember, there is nothing wrong *with a little fun!!*

I have also found that specific sports contests can be played different ways which helps that much-needed variation.

As an example, below is one set of guidelines to **The Football Game,** and a second way to play can be found in Chapter 8.

Announce the game a few weeks prior using your home team (college or pro) and the appropriate upcoming opponent.

Divide the scheduled TSR's into the two teams advising them in advance who they will be playing for. This will allow them to wear the appropriate colors of their team on game day. These pregame activities are used for both ways of playing.

Here are the rules for one way of playing **Football:**

- Timewise, divide the shift into halves, with break time representing half time.

- As TSR's reach calling goals, they produce offensive yardage toward "touchdowns" worth seven points each.

- Two penalties (incorrectly filled out orders, incomplete presentations, etc.) on either team rewards the opposing team a "field goal" (three points).

- The highest scoring team at shift's end is the winner and is awarded pizza the following week.

- The MVP (player with the most offensive yardage on either team) is awarded a trophy.

Here are a couple of additional ways I added authentic fun to this contest:

- Use a cap gun to end the 1st half and the game.

- Use yellow penalty flags (made from simple yellow fabric).

- Have management, supervisors or verifiers wear referees shirts and use whistles appropriately.

- If possible present the MVP with tickets to the actual game.

Here's another tip to enhance this contest (depending on your contacts it may or may not be possible): Because I was formally a Public Relations Manager for some of the Cincinnati Bengal football players, I was able to have one of my friends who played on the Bengals come in and present the MVP with tickets to the game.

I made the announcement regarding this that evening just prior to "kick off" and it provided additional incentive to produce offensive yardage. Although I had a unique advantage to this exciting visit and presentation by a player, you may find this possible by calling the public relations office of your local team. Explain your team support and see if the possibility exists of having a player come out.

Also note that the MVP can come from either the ultimate winner or losing team as well. This way, TSR energy stays high even if one team goes way ahead during the contest.

Robert Jackson, a Cincinatti Bengals football player, presents the MVP of Dave's TSR Football game with tickets to the Bengals' game.

Other sports ideas can be found in Chapter 8.

One last tip on sports-related contests. They are most successful when affiliated with very visible events such as season openers, all star games, playoff games, the World Series, Super Bowl, Masters, the U.S. Open, and other widely-publicized events.

Use Culture to Develop Contest Themes

Earlier I mentioned culture as a potential theme for contests.

For example, the 1950's and 1960's seem to be one of the most nostalgic times in the history of our country. The music .... with American Rock & Roll and the British invasion .... muscle cars .... major influences from the world of entertainment .... the tragic loss of prominent political figures ..... the war in Viet Nam, even players and moments in sports that will never be forgotten make these two decades a favorite among many people.

Being an enthusiastic fan of this era myself, I developed a contest that whenever used pays high motivational dividends and increases productivity.

The rules to my **50's-60's Day** can be found in Chapter 8. If you decide to implement this contest or something similar, put together a promotional flyer for your employees a week or so prior to your visit to the past. Once again, this pre-contest hype will add to the anticipation and ultimate success of a contest such as this.

Another favorite era of the past to bring back seems to be the 1920's and 30's.

Whatever time period you use, remember, you are trying to reach all the different motivational buttons of your people. Vary the themes of your contests. Running the same contests over and over again will not turn on everyone and will even become redundant and ineffective for those who once enjoyed them.

Even I, probably the world's most addicted "Chocoholic," must have a diversified diet when it comes to my fix. The same candy bar over and over becomes uninteresting and unstimulating. Change the name and ingredients and, *WOW*, what a difference!

How Long Should Contests Last?

Variation in contest length is essential to maintain a high TSR interest level in your contests.

Once again, the same contest or even different contests that always last one day or always last three days or always last one week will become boring based on predictability and redundancy.

People need *variety!*

Altering the length of your contests should be very easy. After all, *you're* the one designing them! Make some of your contests last two months . . . . others only four hours, and many in-between.

Wait a minute! Did I say *two months?*

Yes, I did.

And I know what you're thinking . . . . and you're right. The *longer* a contest lasts the *harder* it is to maintain the motivation linked to it.

This is true. But the last time I looked in a thesaurus "impossible" was not a synonym of "harder."

Don't be like many managers and be afraid to try a longer contest. The key to making it work is implementing a collection of short-term contests within the expanded time frame of the long one.

The "TSR Action Auction"

As an example let's look at a long-term contest and then set up a hypothetical game plan for some short-term stimulation in-between.

When I developed the **TSR Action Auction** back in 1986, I was told it would never work because "it was too long." Not only did it work that first time, but everytime I have used it in any environment it has been highly successful.

Here are the rules and a few tips for success:

- Select a two- or three-month time window for this contest and announce a start date and an auction date.

- Calling goals and associated cash values are then announced to the TSR's.

- As TSR's reach calling goals, simulated currency is awarded on a daily or weekly basis.

- Bonus "cash" can be awarded for additional goals, such as perfect attendance and exceeding performance levels.

- On **Auction Day** employees use accumulated "cash" to bid on prizes (company logo items, movie passes, dinner certificates, small appliances, etc.).

- Prior to contest kickoff, present a list of all prizes or display them for TSR's to view.

- The head manager should act as auctioneer on **Auction Day.**

Two further tips: don't use plain Monopoly money, and, log your payouts!

Allow one of my painful memories from the past to help you. (Oh, how we live and learn!) The first time I ran the **Action Auction** I handed out Monopoly money — foolishly I might add — for the first two days until I realized that people seemed to have accumulated *more* cash than I had handed out.

It finally occurred to me that they were supplementing their daily take with money from their *own* Monopoly games at home. In fact, I later learned that two TSR's had even gone out and *bought new Monopoly games* just to use the money! What an education I got!

It didn't take long for me to fix this situation, and here are my recommendations for simulated currency in this or any contest:

- purchase a unique ink stamp and use it on every bill in the same place prior to distribution.

- initial every bill prior to distribution.

- create a contest log with all employee names on it.

- document all money distributions to all TSR's.

This way when you get to auction day and someone is bidding $300 on a prize and you have them logged in for only $200 .... you know what I mean.

Now to the game plan for shorter contests to help sustain the interest levels during the **Action Auction.**

How to Keep Interest Levels High During Long Contests
What I have done each time I run this auction is implement either the **Money Hat** or the **Who, What, or Where** posters on an every-week or every-other-week basis. Other short-term contests will be equally effective here, and make sure the award for these additional contests is more cash for the auction itself. This will help your people keep the main contest in focus, maintaining stimulation over the long haul.

Contest Differences Between Inbound and Outbound

Outbound and inbound operations can be very similar when it comes to contest creativity.

Whenever I talk to friends who run inbound operations, the subject of contests is always included. And we always reach the same conclusion: Even though there is a great contrast in function between the two, most of the same contests work in both inbound adn outbound environments.

Remember, contests are based around goals. Once you establish those goals it is easy to apply creative surroundings to enhance productivity. You can use the same contest idea and simply structure it around your specific function. **The Money Hat, Who, What or Where** posters, and the **Football** contests are currently being utilized with equal success in both arenas.

And these are only a few examples. As you choose some favorite ideas later on in Chapter 8, use creative flexibility to adapt them to your environment.

What About Business-to-Consumer and Business-to-Business?

Some of your answers to "Which contests work best?" may depend on which of these two worlds you operate.

In some cases it will make a difference; in others, it won't. Managing offices in both environments has been a very resourceful education for me. What typically motivates part-time professionals in business-to-consumer offices can be far different from the full-time salaried professional in a business-to-business atmosphere.

Age can be a factor here as well. In many consumer operations it is very typical to employ a high percentage of younger people: high school and college students, young housewives and even younger couples working a second job to make ends meet.

Turn the clock back for a moment to your younger days. (Hopefully you will not need to go back as far as me!) *Time* to do what we wanted to do was a cherished item wasn't it? It was . . . . and still is, and that's why time off is a tremendous motivator in these environments.

During my time at *USA Today*, 80% of my staff of 100 + was this wonderful age that we'd all like to be again. These TSR's worked harder for time off rewards than anything else . . . . *including cash!*

In contrast, corporate and other business-to-business environments usually employ a higher percentage of what I call "more settled professionals." These people are usually older, more experienced . . . . . more focused on making a living to support themselves or a family and to move up in the business world.

Although time off works in almost all environments with any age, business-to-business reps are more motivated by cash and other dollar and cents-driven contests.

There will always be exceptions in both worlds. What is true today may not be true tomorrow. What works in one area may not in another. Be prepared to be flexible to your peoples' needs.

Vary the Way You RUN Your Contests

Even the way you run your contests may vary. Let's look at **The Money Hat** again. In a business-to-consumer operation with a high percentage of younger TSRs this is a fun concept. And it works! And although it may hold true on some business-to-business environments, you may find that some professionals in these settings don't want to wear a little hat in front of everyone.

That's OK. The concept is still effectively implemented by simply changing the **Hat** to a more conservative method of passing the money. This can be accomplished by framing a $5 bill, or using magnified simulated currency you can purchase at novelty stores. The contest rules stay the same and remain effective, but your employees may be more comfortable using a different approach to "passing the buck."

Some contests will work without changes regardless of the application. However, remember that not all contests will automatically work in every environment. Alter your contests based on your needs, make necessary modifications, and most of all, *be creative!*

Again we go back to: once you know what motivates your people you can create your contests based on your knowledge. So, to revisist the question we started this chapter with, "Which contests work best?", the answer is . . . . .

. . . . . the kind that work for *your people* in *your environment*.

Different contests utilizing different themes and methods lasting different lengths of time with different rewards and prizes. All those "differents" equal one thing: *variation.*

4. How and When To Run Contests

How do you run a contest in a telemarketing environment?

That's a very general question..... one I'm asked quite frequently when I deliver speeches and presentations across North America. And there's no simple answer. That's because there are several other key questions that play a part in the success of the contest:

- When should you implement contests and how often should you have them?

- What should the calling goals be?

- Who should be involved supervising contests?

- Who should win?

- Who *shouldn't* win?

The answers to these questions play a critical role in determining the success of a motivational game plan that includes contests. Let's address them individually.

Contest Timing

When is the most successful time to run a contest? How often should contests be implemented? The answers to these questions are not simple and are, for the most part, inconsistent.

Some strongly believe that if you have a contest that's working, go to the well until it dries up or continue to run that contest until people are tired of it.

Others, including myself, emphatically believe that this overexposure of any contest is not the best way, based on the fact that telephone sales professionals need a varied menu of contests to be most effective. I'm sure that in some cases both of these theories have worked.

For instance, my audiences always have at least one manager who claims success by what is called "running a contest to death." These people typically bring up the old phrases such as "If it ain't broke don't fix it," or "Don't mess with success."

But, *is it success?*

Just as much as I believe you must vary the themes of your contests, I also believe you must vary the *timing*.

In most cases, running a short-term contest day after day until people get tired of it *will* run it literally to death. Some people will lose their interest in that contest forever, and, more importantly, as the days during the contest pass, the excitement surrounding it will diminish.

THINK ABOUT IT!

It won't go from total excitement one day to the tired-out phase the very next day. Nor will this be a sudden change at anytime during the contest. There is a period of time where peoples' feelings about a contest will gradually decline, and with this loss of enthusiasm comes diminishing returns.

An Example of an Overworked Contest

Years ago I had to revive **The Money Hat** from near-extinction after almost running it into the ground.

It was new. It was exciting. It worked. So I continued to use only that contest day after day until someone woke me up with the following words, "We're tired of it. What other contest can we have?"

And as I look back, I can remember that after a certain point, the excitement *had* decreased. At the time, I thought it was because

I was only giving out $1. So I changed it to $2 thinking that would regenerate the enthusiasm.

NOT SO!

It wasn't the money! It was how *often* I was running the contest. My TSRs were simply tired of the concept.

After waking up to this fact, it was some time before I used **The Money Hat** again, but as I eased it back into existence, gradually it became popular once again. Thank goodness I hadn't killed it forever because it remains a favorite.

Make Contests Special Events
Also, any contest should be a special event — or at least somewhat of a special event.

Even if you have a huge library of contests to mix up and select from, I don't believe you should run contests every day, or even every week.

Once again, let my education from the "School of Hard Knocks" serve as an example:

As Assistant Telemarketing Manager in a *USA Today* regional office, I was just getting started in the telemarketing business. I went with the theory of running contests all the time. Like any manager, I wanted the highest sales possible from my office. What I failed to take into account was the human element. At least not until I realized that the contests in our office were no longer a special event. In fact, the worst scenario had occurred: they were now an expectation.

They had gone from being what they should be, a luxury or added benefit, to what they shouldn't be, an expectation or necessity.

And it doesn't take long for this to happen. The problem lies in the value of appreciation. It goes down. And when it does, the enthusiasm diminishes somewhat and will be reflected in the plunging results of your TSR's.

It's human nature. When you are exposed to *anything* too often, your appreciation for it becomes almost nonexistent.

To illustrate, change gears with me for a moment and think about a hot fudge sundae . . . . vanilla ice cream packed in perfectly rounded portions in your dish, with hot fudge oozing over the sides with a sprinkling of chopped nuts, fluffy whipped cream and a bright red cherry invitingly topping it off.

Now, if I begin to take my kids out for this sundae every single day I guarantee it won't be long until their appreciation turns into *expectation.*

Will the seventh one in a row mean as much as the first one?

NOT A CHANCE!

They won't enjoy it as much. They'll now take it for granted that we are going for ice cream, and as a result their enthusiasm will have declined, which naturally diminishes the impact.

And so it is with contests in my telemarketing environment and yours.

Leave Them Wanting for More
My office went through a short time of contest withdrawal as I corrected my atmosphere by not running contests every day and turning them back into what they should be, a special event.

And part of that withdrawal was another portion of the human element that becomes evident when running contests too often. When they become expected rather than appreciated, the attitude of your people will be very negative when you don't have one going on. Take it from someone who learned the hard way!

Col. Tom Parker, who was Elvis Presley's manager for many years, often said that part of the magic that surrounded Elvis' popularity was in being careful to not overexpose him. Not spoiling the people with too much. To always "leave the people wanting more."

In order for your contest game plan to maintain maximum impact, use contests during special promotions, during holidays and other themes we looked at in Chapter 3, and sometimes spontaneously. But remember . . . . contests need to be a *special event* — not an everyday occurrence.

Get Management Involved for Best Results

Another key element of successful contests is the participattion of managment. Management involvement is not mandatory for contests to run smoothly or to be successful. However, participation at this level certainly does enhance your staff's perception of the commitment and support of management. For this reason alone, it is a valuable use of time for managers to be involved with contests past the implementation stage.

Although a supervisor may monitor the daily contest activity, a manager's involvement can add an enormous inspirational lift to employees. A manager who periodically gets "involved" with contest happenings will be instrumental in the success level of any contest. For instance, whenever I run the **Action Auction**, I make sure I will be available to be Auctioneer on the day set aside for bidding on prizes. Because they know I am actively involved from the beginning, they become more enthusiastic overall. And so do I!

I have a higher level of interest throughout the contest regarding who's earning money and what prizes people are shooting for. When auction day arrives I'm probably more excited than they are!

And managers . . . . pay close attention here: *make the auction fun!*

Give away a few gag gifts. Have a sense of humor at the microphone.

Also, don't go through the auction too fast. What's the hurry? Nothing. So drag it out a little. Share some fun and exciting office moments that occurred during the contest. Whenever I know I'll be running this contest as auctioneer, I always take notes during the contest period on any "special moments" that occur. Then I share these during the auction. These are always a hoot, and are also the enjoyable times that are etched in your employees' memories when they think of contests (and of course this is what motivates them).

Examples of "special moments" might be someone setting a record for a certain area of productivity. For example, recognize everyone having perfect attendance during the contest. Share some stories from monitoring. I can remember one year I shared a "monitor moment" to open up auction day and it seemed to set the mood for a good time.

Just a week after the contest began, a TSR that I was listening to turned to her neighbor between calls and said, "Can you *believe* the tie that Dave is wearing tonight? It doesn't even go with the shirt he has on!"

Well, here I am still monitoring, only *now* I'm peering down at my tie, wondering to myself, "What's *wrong* with this tie and shirt?"

Right at that point I heard her say, "Oh my gosh!", and I looked up to find her staring at me. She saw that I was on the monitor phone, looking down at my tie and must have realized that I was listening to her. We looked at each other for what seemed like an eternity — both embarrassed — and then both of us broke into laughter.

When I shared this humorous internal story it seemed to set the tone for a great time. And it was!

Use Contests to Promote Manager/Rep Interaction

Every time we put up the **Who, What, or Where Poster Board** I always control the master list of prizes to have close contact with the contest as people get rewarded. This way, anytime they pull off a self-sticking note with a number, they have to see me to find out what prize is associated with that number. This now becomes a perfect opportunity for praise from me, which will additionally stimulate the employee.

Football and other sports event contests present one of the best opportunities for managers to be involved and play a truly active role enhancing the contest. As a team Coach or possibly the Referee, there is high visibility of management commitment to the reps which will further energize them. If possible, also get senior level executives involved. In Chapter 1, we talked about executive recognition and the enormous impact it can have in our efforts to create and maintain a positive atmosphere in our telemarketing environments.

This is a golden opportunity to be creative and find ways to involve upper management in some portions of contests. Some ideas for possible involvement include:

1) **CONTEST KICK OFF:** The day you begin a contest have a member of top management boost the enthusiasm with a few opening remarks related to the contest itself or the performance goals associated with the contest. For example, if you are playing **TSR Football,** the executive could announce the teams and blow the whistle to begin the game with the opening kick-off.

Have them pass out **The Money Hat** to the TSR with the first sale when implementing that contest. Depending on the contest you are running, there are many different ways of opening it up. BE CREATIVE!

2) **PRESENTATION OF POST-CONTEST PRIZE/AWARDS:** Anytime an executive physically performs a presentation of awards or contest prizes it seems to carry an enormous amount of stimulation with it. To be rewarded by *anyone* in front of your co-workers is exciting . . . . but when you are rewarded in front of peers by senior management it carries a certain special meaning.

In fact, that's an understatement; the value *skyrockets!*

When you run the **Action Auction,** see if you can get an executive to hand out the prizes as employees bid on them. The manager as auctioneer and an executive handing out prizes paints a beautiful picture of management involvement. And although role-reversal is possible (the executive as auctioneer and you handing out prizes), I don't recommend it. You'll be missing that ingredient of one-on-one between your employees and an executive. Any contest that involves prizes or rewards at the end is an excellent time to involve a senior level executive.

3) **SPONTANEOUS VISITS:** Regardless of what contest you are running, spontaneous involvement by senior management will have an extremely positive impact on your employees.

Ask someone from upper management to stop by during **The Money Hat** and have them ring the bell and hand out money or present TSR's with prizes when they pull a number note off the **Who, What, Or Where Poster Board.** Maybe they could keep score for one-half of **TSR Football**, acting as a cheerleader or interim coach. Have them stop by and pass out shamrocks for an hour during the **St. Patrick's Day Pot-O-Gold** or act as Santa Claus during a Christmas contest.

How long does this list go on? As long as you can make it.

Remember, it is normal to press harder to succeed in front of management. Whenever possible, managers should initiate that extra effort by getting involved and showing their commitment.

Don't be surprised if you — and your bosses — end up having as much fun as your TSR's! And remember, find a way to get VP's, Presidents and other top level management to see the benefit of their brief involvement. A small investment of their time here will bring huge returns in motivation.

The Authentic Atmosphere

Picture the area that your telephone professionals work in every day. You've decided to implement a contest based on the 1950's and 60's. Now let's jump in our fictional time capsule and drift off for a few moments . . . .

. . . . . bubble-top juke boxes, soda fountains, the Beatles, a '57 Chevy with foam dice hanging from the mirror, poodle skirts, Mickey Mantle, High School letter sweaters, Elvis, 6 oz. Cokes, James Dean, penny loafers, Woodstock, Leave It To Beaver, the Peace symbol, Joe Namath . . . . .

. . . . . the list goes on and on, but we must return to reality.

But wait!

Wouldn't it be great to bring some of that era back with us for our contest? Can we? Should we?

YES it would, *YES* we can, and, *YES* we should!

Whenever possible (and practical) use any props which will help set the mood for the contest. For a very nominal fee you can purchase some large cardboard cutouts affiliated with the 50's/60's. Where do you find these things? Normally you can purchase these types of items at carnival wholesale companies or novelty stores. They typically cost $1-$3. Tape these on the walls or hang them from the ceiling. Put up a poster of the Beatles or Elvis and hang a set of foam dice from the ceiling. Have your people dress appropriately when the day of the contest arrives.

With minimal expense – but with creative imagination – you can enhance any contest by creating this authentic atmosphere.

Depending on the contest, this can be done well before the day of the contest or on the day itself. Creating this atmosphere will assist in energizing your employees prior to, and during, any contest. Whenever you do something additional to pump up the excitement and anticipation of your telephone professionals, their performance level will naturally escalate accordingly.

Since most holidays are good times to implement contests and should be a natural time to display appropriate decorations in your area, it is easy to create the right atmosphere at holiday times.

And whether or not you run a contest on holidays, I highly recommend appropriate decorations around *all holidays.* In general it helps everyone's attitude and I think we agree on how important a positive attitude is in our industry of business by phone.

Because this can usually be a very inexpensive way to add high energy to your environment, it will be one of your highest paybacks when you look at expense vs. impact.

Who Should And Shouldn't Win

Predetermined winners can turn a great contest idea and a lot of work into a quick disaster. The predetermined winner usually emerges as a result of an unintentional mistake by the contest creator when determining call goals for the contest. If everyone knows who will win before the contest begins, you will lose any chance of meeting the objective you want and ultimately will demotivate your people. In every telemarketing environment I know of there are different levels of achievers.

The purpose of any contest is for *everyone* to improve their productivity for reward while stimulating their overall morale. If a contest is set up to reward only one winner who is the person with the most sales, appointments or similar criteria, top achievers will be the only ones with a chance to win. Those individuals will immediately be perceived (correctly) by everyone else as the predetermined winners. At this point the contest has failed. The additional effort you needed from everyone is now limited to only those that know they have a realistic chance to win. Overall attitude will also be negatively affected which is counterproductive to the entire atmosphere. When I began to develop and implement some of my first contests in a telemarketing environment, I made those mistakes but quickly learned from them.

How a Predetermined Winner Meant Contest Disaster

Our office was responsible for newspaper subscriptions being generated by three separate groups placing different call types: A renewal of an existing customer, the restart of a former subscriber, and the cold call for a new subscriber. The renewal was by far the easiest sale, with former subscribers next and, naturally, the cold call was by far the most difficult.

When designing my first few contests, I arbitrarily (but unknowingly) chose sales numbers that would be most quickly attained by TSR's working on renewal subscriptions. Obviously this was unintentional, but intent was irrelevant to the results.

It was a disaster.

The people working renewals *knew* they would win. And worse, the others working cold calls also knew the renewal callers would win. The attitudes of the cold-callers became negative toward the contest, and their jealousy of work assignments further provoked their feelings. A very unsuccessful contest was underway.

Using my 20/20 hindsight, *of course* the TSR's working renewals would get the most sales. Wake up and smell the coffee, Dave!

Let my bad experience be a learning tool for you; analyze the chances of winning your contest from the eyes of your TSR's — especially just-average performers — and be sure they have a fair chance of winning something.

Another One That's Sure to Fail

Let another one of my contests-gone-sour be a helpful lesson:

Whenever you set up a contest to reward just one TSR for reaching a goal first, more times than not, the contest stands little chance of overall success.

I made this mistake — twice — before I realized how counter-productive it was.

Like you, I was not equipped with a crystal ball and could not predict when the winner would emerge victorious. Our shift ran from 5:00 p.m. to 10:00 p.m., and the first night someone won at 7:45, therefore ending the contest. The next night it ended at 7:30 when a TSR won with a certain amount of sales. An interesting development was that probably an hour or so prior to the contest conclusion many of my people had given up based on their sales at the time and how far behind the contest leader they were.

So, one and one-half hours into the contest, many TSR's had quit striving, and the contest was all but formally over by 7:30-7:45 .. ... consequently taking the wind from the sails for the rest of the evening.

Productive? About as productive as filling a bucket that has a gaping hole in it!

I later ran the same contest when I rewarded *every* TSR who reached the predetermined goal with a prize. As a way to assure an enthusiastic start, an additional prize went to the *first three* to reach that goal. It was so much more successful. This way even if the first three had reached the goals by 7:30, everyone else still had a chance to win by reaching the goal at later times. Therefore, everyone was still motivated to push throughout the evening.

Reward Multiple Winners
The need to succeed is alive in all of us. Everyone needs to know they have an opportunity to win for any contest to be successful. Because of this need, develop most of your contests to reward multiple winners or teams.

For example, in some cases you can even design programs to reward everyone equally. To accomplish this I have used time off with pay for the prize, which is always a high motivator in this profession.

Calculate your average shift activity per half hour and add that total to the overall performance number affiliated with a full shift of work. Increase that number by 10-25% and give your employees that goal to reach. If they achieve that as a team, everyone receives a half-hour credit of free time to be used anytime they want. Everyone wins here. The rationale is that if performance exceeds normal levels, the company wins. The TSR's have a great time earning free time so they win, and you as a manager or supervisor win doubly. You increase productivity and profits while building a positive atmosphere. You can also escalate the reward to one hour and follow the same guidelines. The key is to make sure that the final goal you establish pays back beyond the free time you give out.

Another system for making sure everyone has an opportunity to win is to simply use previous call history for each individual and increase all their productivity goals by an equal percentage. Anyone exceeding their expanded goal wins. Everyone has the opportunity to win, but not everyone *will* necessarily win. This is the type of contest that can also reward one person above and beyond the rest and still be very effective. With the same rules in effect, the person with the highest percentage over their average performance earns a grand prize.

It is imperative for the self esteem of your people and the overall atmosphere of your telemarketing environment that different people win contests. It is equally important that the perception of predetermined winners is nonexistent in your surroundings.

Determining Call Goals

Deciding on what call goals need to be reached to determine contest winners is often overlooked in regards to the performance impact you are expecting. Don't make this fatal mistake!

Usually contest goals are established in order to escalate typical call numbers, and to consequently make that new level the benchmark for success during the course of the contest. This *can be* effective at times .... when your goal is to simply increase your overall numbers. However, if you *limit* your objective to merely inflating general productivity, you will miss out on golden opportunities that can positively affect your employees, while at the same time escalating their performance and your company's profits.

Contests can also have a substantial impact on your environment when utilized to enhance training efforts and specific telephone techniques or to support particular company goals. Psychological experts agree that any behavior repeated on a regular basis becomes a habit in three weeks.

Create contests with very specific goals that will help turn good basic fundamentals of your telemarketing professionals into solid habits. For example, let's say you want to create a contest to support your training of answering objections. For the next three weeks you could develop some contests that exclusively reward those individuals who properly address objections during the course of their calling activity. Your staff would then focus on this important technique. Through concentration and regular performance, your TSR's will begin to habitually address objections based on your needs, therefore, enhancing their productivity levels.

You could also have periodic training targeted to enhance product knowledge. Design contests that specifically incent the TSR's who show strong product knowledge while speaking with customers and prospects. Run these contests for three consecutive weeks to help permanently strengthen your staff's memory bank regarding your company's products and/or services.

These are only two examples among many possibilities. Create contests to support any areas of specific training and other important telephone techniques such as presentations, listening skills, closing techniques and probing skills.

Make Your Goals Realistic

The most critical element in deciding on call goals for any contest is making sure that the GOALS ARE ACHIEVABLE.

A manager's wish list in terms of increased performance can sometimes become exaggerated or unrealistic. Your reps will be able to recognize unreachable goals early into a contest. When this happens, double damage occurs. Number one, the impact of the immediate contest will dramatically diminish. Number two, you will have inadvertently set the tone for TSR disbelief when it comes time for future contests.

Then, every time you introduce a contest, eyes will roll and reps will mutter questions under their breath to each other about whether the goals are even attainable. Just the *perception* of unrealistic goals will lessen the overall impact of any contest.

Therefore, while your goals should be very challenging, they need to be at the same time indisputably reachable.

We've taken a good look at:

- When to run your contests and how often.

- How you as managers need to be involved (and how to involve upper-managent).

- How to determine calling goals.

- Who should and shouldn't win.

- How to create the authentic atmosphere.

Now we need to focus on what prizes to reward our people with, and we'll do that in the next chapter.

5. Contest Incentives

How important is the prize or reward that your TSRs receive for winning contests? Is it more important than the contest itself?

Let's jump in our time capsules again and go back to our breakfast tables on a Saturday morning:

> Mom had usually gone grocery shopping on Friday night . . . . and what did that mean for Saturday morning? A new box of cereal! And if you were like me, the cereal itself was somewhat insignificant. Most cereals are good, but only some have prizes inside. And that's what I looked for first. And do I mean *look!*

Think of all the different ways we use to try to find the prizes . . .

Remember jamming your hand down through the box — crushing the cereal on the way — just to see if you could feel your way to the prize? I sure do! Or how about pressuring the box from the sides, enlarging the opening enough to peek further down the sides as you gently shook the box? And if these tactics didn't work, I'm sure at one time or another we all performed the final act: dumping the cereal out on the counter or in a large bowl until we could get the prize out.

All this effort! And for what? Not what you would call collector's items.

In most cases, they were — and still are — extremely inexpensive items. Things that we played with for about five minutes and then tossed aside until our mothers cleaned the closet. Yet, the intense effort to get to those cereal box prizes will always exist.

How important was the prize?

Not very.

It was the *challenge* to get to it. The competitiveness in us that wants to accomplish something . . . . anything.

I have found the same theory to hold true with most contests. As we discussed in Chapter 2, competition is the driving factor — not the prize.

But, certainly the prize itself does carry some value, so let's look at some ideas to be used for contest prizes.

Variety By Theme

Once again, variation is the key. A variety of prizes is necessary for maximum stimulation. Giving away dinner certificates every time will soon make your contests ineffective because some people will not continue to be motivated for the same prize over and over. Some people like brunch more than dinner. Others might prefer movie passes . . . . or tickets to sports events . . . . or bowling certificates . . . . and the list goes on and on.

One way to effectively mix up your prize ideas is to affiliate the prizes with contest themes as much as possible. So as you develop different contest ideas, think in advance about what might be the perfect prizes associated with the contest theme. Here are some examples that I use.

Remember the 50's/60's contests? The first time I ran this contest, I gave away $25 to the winner. Cash, the ultimate motivator, right?

WRONG!

The contest was more fun when the prizes were affiliated with the 50's/60's. Some of the prize ideas that I used to successfully enhance this contest are:

- Lunch or dinner certificates to a local 50's/60's restaurant. (Hard Rock Cafe, Heartthrob Cafe.) If these are not locally accessible, find a diner or other restaurant with this theme.

- Cassette tapes or albums of classic oldies. Everyone has some favorite from that era!

- Tickets to a concert put on by some of the artists from either the 50's/60's. Many of these individuals and groups are touring once again much to the delight of millions.

- Entries to a 50's/60's night club. Since this is usually a minimal fee, also add some spending money.

- A radio or tape player that resembles an old bubbletop juke box.

Or for the **Pot-O-Gold** contest, use one of the following two prizes:

- A small black pot filled with chocolate coins covered in gold foil.

- Give three winners (representing the third month, March) a small black pot filled with $17 (representing the date, the 17th) in assorted change.

When you play the **TSR Football Game** we talked about in Chapter 3, give the MVP one of the following:

- Tickets to the game involving the teams your contest simulated.

- An article of clothing with your home team logo on it. (Sweatshirts, T-shirts, jackets, or hats make great gifts.

- An autographed football from your local team. Contact the public relations department of your team and tell them about your contest and ask about the possibility of purchasing an autographed football.

Prizes awarded to the winning astronauts in **Journey to the Moon** were dinner certificates to the Blue *Moon* saloon and tickets to *Moon* Glow Tanning spa. Second place got tickets to the movie Space Balls.

These are only some examples of contest theme prizes and I am sure many more would surface with further creative thinking.

There isn't a contest you can create that doesn't have possibilities for theme-associated prizes and rewards. Whenever possible I strongly recommend these contest affiliated prizes.

The Point System

I briefly mentioned in Chapter 1 that I used a catalog company as part as a commission structure for my TSR's. It operates on a point system that allows employees to accumulate points used to "pay" for gifts selected out of a catalog.

This system is fabulous for contests because the TSR's are always looking for ways to increase their point totals in order to pick out more elaborate gifts. The best part of this system is that points can be used at anytime for any accomplishment during the contest, or for the final prize at the end of a contest.

A perfect example would involve the **Who, What, or Where Poster Board**. Whenever I run this contest, my point system plays a major role in the prizes. For the master list that represents 25-40% of the self-sticking notes, I use different point values as prizes. Since each point represents one-half a cent, I put up many different amounts. Such as 400 points ($2), 500 points ($2.50), 750 points ($3.75), 1000 points ($5) and every so often I will put one number that equals 2000 points ($10). At the end of the contest I will occasionally use points as the grand prize as well.

My people preferred the point system over cash because it allows them the opportunity to have something they might not purchase otherwise. We all know how cash can simply slip through our fingers with little to show for it.

The company I use for this great system is Olsen O'Leary Associates/Travel Incorporated, Market Motivation Specialists, 565 Epsilon Drive, Pittsburg, PA, 15238, (412)963-7272. If you contact them, they will put you in touch with a local representative or deal with you on a direct basis. They offer a fabulous catalog with prizes for every possible dream that anyone could have.

Time Off

This is one of my personal favorites. Why?

Because it works!

Having managed operations in both the business-to-consumer and business-to-business worlds, I have seen this prize of time off be equally important to TSR's in both arenas. It is a stronger motivator in the business-to-consumer world based on the typical profile of the telephone professionals.

Why does time off work so well?

Let's begin answering that by looking at our industry for a brief moment. It is certainly one that drives quicker burnout than most, therefore, making time away from the phone more valuable to your people. And I know what you may be thinking: "Is this guy nuts? I'm not in business to let my people get *away* from the phone. They need to be on the phone all the time."

Not so.

Number one, I am not talking about week-long vacations here.

Number two, if your goals are set properly, the productivity you expected above and beyond the norm has been met, so how can this be bad?

Because of the high level of burnout, minimal amounts of time off carry a huge value with telemarketing professionals. Depending on the contest I am running, most of my prizes of time off range anywhere from 15 minutes, to one hour. Occasionally there has been up to a half-day off. But that's rare, since I can get the same motivational effect with smaller pieces of time. A little bit stretches a long way!

To represent time, I have used Monopoly money in the proper denominations. Or simply a written note designating the appropriate time off.   But the best item I have found to date is a large plastic simulated quarter. I hand out these quarters to represent one quarter-hour or 15 minutes of free time. Once again, local novelty wholesalers are your best bet to find these plastic quarters.

Examples of How to Use Time Off
Here are three examples of how I use time off when given as a prize during or following a contest.

1. Extended or additional breaks. If you are asking, "Breaks? What breaks?", strongly consider my next recommendation: If you don't currently have scheduled breaks, for every four-hour shift there should be a minimum of a 15-minute break involved. In this profession it is definitely needed, and, in most cases (I hope), much deserved. Use the free quarters we spoke of earlier to enhance their breaks by extending them 15 minutes or giving out extra breaks.

2. Extended lunch. This idea is geared for the business-to-business arena based on full-time employees who usually work 8-5 with lunch squeezed in somewhere. In the world of business-to-consumer the shifts typically run four to five hours, and are of a part time nature, so this opportunity will not usually exist here. Once again, the free quarters can be used here as well as other time off prizes including one-half hour or even one hour. Any of you familiar with having 60 minutes for lunch can certainly identify with the many times we all wished it were just a little longer. A lunch break is a perfect time to allow additional free time based on reaching productivity goals in a contest.

3. Early dismissal/late arrival. Time off can be used in any environment involving an early dismissal from work or a late arrival to work. In fact, this has always has been a favorite use of free quarters for my people.

The concept of delaying your arrival by even 15 minutes means a great deal to most telephone professionals. It translates into a few more minutes of sleep before getting up, or some extra time of afternoon fun if you work a night shift.

The same holds true for an early dismissal. If cornered for the most popular use of time off, I would say this is it. There is something extra special about having the option of leaving work early.

Once again, I think we would agree there are times that we would all like to have that option. More than that, I know with little effort we can all think of past times it would have been great to get off even 15 minutes to a half-hour early. A day you were leaving on vacation or had tickets to a ballgame or going out to dinner . . . . and the list goes on.

These are the times that a little time means a great deal. And your payback as a manager should be there as well. That's why you need to make sure as you set your call goals for a contest that your return exceeds the value of the prize. It's alright to let your reps off the phone at times if they have earned it by achieving totals during contests that they would not normally reach.

Since I initiated my very first contest, time off remains the favorite prize, by far, among my employees.

Outside Seminars

One prize I occasionally use is attendance to outside seminars that are affiliated with telephone techniques. Even though I am not talking about extremely expensive registration fees, it is still somewhat costly to do this. However, the payback usually outweighs the expense. It is always a stimulating break for anyone to go off-site for a seminar for the day. Not only are you away from the office but there is a certain prestige attached. The key here is to have all of your employees win when having only one person go to the seminar. Let the winning employee know ahead of time that you would like them to do a brief seminar presentation to all their co-workers upon return from the seminar. This way everyone benefits from one person attending. This also acts as a stimulant for the winning employee who gets a leadership role in front of their peers. (And as a side benefit, you get a training program delivered that you don't have to prepare yourself.)

Movie Passes/Dinner Certificates

Although these are age-old prizes, they remain effective. Most people — regardless of age — enjoy a night out for dinner, a movie, or both.

Movie passes should be certificates and not tickets to a specific film. Remember, what excites one person does not necessarily work for another. Don't ruin the prize impact by giving out tickets to a movie that the winner doesn't even want to see. *Let them choose!*

I've also found that many times movie theaters will give you two tickets to any film if you agree to spend x-amount of dollars at the concession stand.

I try to make a deal everytime I need movie tickets to use as a prize. I will talk to the manager on duty, explain the contest and make the following offer: I'll agree to spend $5 at the concession stand in exchange for two tickets to give away as prizes. Sometimes it works . . . . other times it doesn't. But how do you know until you *ask*? Keep in mind that the concession stand is where theaters make their money. Or at least it better be. Think about those prizes!

Dinner certificates have always been a popular prize based on two factors. Number one, there are so many great restaurants to choose from that you can always satisfy anyone and everyone's tastebuds, and, number two, let's face it, *we all love to eat!*

Movie passes and dinner certificates will always appeal to people. Therefore, they will always be safe, popular prizes.

Company Logo Premiums

Items with company logos have quickly become one of the most popular reward or prize ideas. T-shirts, polo shirts, hats, umbrellas, keychains, duffle bags, golf balls . . . . the list goes on and on. Most people feel proud to wear the company colors, especially when it represents a prize that is won in a contest.

Think about it. It has become a status symbol for your peers to see you sporting your company logo on something you won in a contest. In most cases it will be one of the most supportive prizes by upper management. They love to see people walk around displaying the company logo.

Many times at *USA Today* and Diebold I have used this idea to reward winners of contests. And as much as I use it, the impact of the idea never seems to diminish. One contest that seems to be particularly good for these items is the **TSR Action Auction**. Each time I run this contest, company logo premiums are about 25-30% of the prizes.

Lottery Tickets

This is a new one for me and what a powerful prize! If your state has a lottery, I strongly recommend this idea. The best part about this prize is your return on investment. It is very inexpensive and extremely effective, giving you a high yield on a small investment.

I will go out and buy 20 tickets for $20 and use them while playing the **Money Hat** or other one-shift or one-day contests.

The chance to win millions of dollars excites everyone! It brings out a fantasy that we all have . . . . thinking about how it would feel, what we would spend it on, how we would share it and so on.

This idea usually works best when used as close to the lottery drawing day as possible. That's when the media begins to build it up, people in stores are buying tickets, and colleagues are talking about it at work.

I have often been asked "Does it work the next time even though no one wins the lottery?" In all the times I have used this as the prize, I don't think any one of my employees has even matched just two of the six numbers required to win the lottery. Although no one has come close to winning, the excitement is always at a maximum when lottery tickets are at stake. That dream . . . . that fantasy of winning will always be inside people. Most people who pay to play the lottery (maybe even some of your TSR's) never cash a ticket. Yet that doesn't deter their habit of doling out their dollars week after week. You can stimulate that same feeling and bring it to surface by offering lottery tickets as a reward.

I usually double-stick them to a poster board and put the board up in a very visible spot, allowing winning TSRs to choose the lottery tickets accordingly. These are a must prize for all environments — especially those with limited budgets.

Status Symbols

In this case the perception of value is the critical ingredient. Think about the commercials on television for Pillsbury that feature that fluffy little doughboy. I wrote to Pillsbury and purchased a seven-inch tall figurine of the famous Pillsbury doughboy and I use this as a status symbol in my department. If you are thinking "Who cares about a little doughboy?" . . . . remember we are talking about *perception* of value. I have presented this doughboy as a symbol of power. Something to claim ownership of and display proudly in your area.

I will have a contest for a day, and the person bringing in the most "dough" during that day gets the status of claiming the doughboy for display in his/her area. They hold control over him until this contest is run again. A power struggle begins again to gain control of this little figurine of the Pillsbury doughboy.

My newest item is a small replica of the Energizer Bunny with the drum that keeps interrupting commercials on TV. Give this to the person who simply keeps going and going and going and going.

Some of the others I mentioned in Chapter 1 include the California Raisin for the person during a contest that has the highest percentage of "raisin" his or her performance level over the previous day, week, etc.

Here's another I found during the course of my normal travels. I was in Hollywood on a recent trip to speak in Los Angeles and I picked up an inexpensive replica of the coveted Oscar that stands about eight inches tall. On any given day I will establish call goals, run a contest, and at day's end present this Oscar to the day's "best producer." Again, this can remain in the winner's area until the next time we run a similar contest.

Your people know it's a "jungle out there," so appreciate that it's a jungle and use a plastic replica of a lion to be placed in the area of the rep considered "king of the jungle" based on calling productivity. A stuffed animal of a lion will work equally well.

These are only some examples of ideas to use as status symbols. Put your thinking caps on when you are out shopping. Looking for new prize ideas has become part of my shopping objective. The toy store has become *my* stop instead of for my children. I am truely a kid in a candy store when I visit one of these toy outlets and go crazy trying to find new concepts for prizes!

Remember, if you can develop the perception by your people that these are status symbols, they will be worth a literal fortune in motivation.

What About Using Cash?

Notice any trend here? Have we even talked about cash? Only briefly for the **Pot-O-Gold** contest early in the chapter. That's because it's not the greatest motivator in many cases. Don't misunderstand. I realize and agree that cash is and always will be effective when used as prizes. But it is not the only — or the best — prize in many situations and with many people.

Non-monetary prizes and rewards such as those we looked at in this chapter can be so much more effective than the almighty dollar.

And, far more important than the actual prize is the challenge you present your people to reach it. It has been my experience that most people will work as hard to win a candy bar as they will a $20 bill.

So managers, stretch out your mind and start brainstorming, because the list of prize ideas is truly endless. You simply need to be creative.

6. 10 Tips For Successful Contests

In previous chapters we looked at why contests work, what contests work best, how and when to implement contests, and how to reward the winners of contests.

We know that not all contests will be effective in every telesales or telemarketing situation, and that some contests can *only* succeed in very specific telemarketing environments.

However, in this chapter, I would like to share what I believe — based on my experience — to be the 10 Tips that will help make contests successful in any telephone environment.

10 TIPS

1) Run Frequent Short-term Contests And Only An Occasional Long-term Contest.

Remember what we talked about in Chapter 3? The longer a contest lasts the harder it is to maintain the stimulation attached to it.

That is why I stress that long-term contests should take place on an infrequent basis.

And the worst mistake you can make is to *only* run long-term contests!

Good ideas that are stretched out too far in length become counterproductive for your TSR's. Take **The Money Hat** for instance. Let's review the rules:

Management sets undisclosed times when it will ring the bell. The TSR that has earned the right to wear **The Money Hat** by achieving specific calling goals is then rewarded. As recommended in Chapter 3, 15 rings could be worth $1 each, or five rings at $3 each, or even three rings worth $5. This has always been a one-day contest run periodically throughout the year.

Can you imagine stretching this out to a month or even a week?

Picture yourself telling your TSR's, "I will be ringing the bell 15 times in the next month and whoever has the hat on wins." I promise your **Money Hat** would quickly lose its motivational luster.

One of the biggest reasons telemarketing managers and supervisors run too many long-term contests is to escape the time and creativity necessary to serve a different menu of contest ideas.

It's much easier right? That is, to implement contests that last six months so you don't have to worry about creating new and different ones every week or month?

Sure it's easier . . . .

. . . . . and also much less stimulating for your TSR's, and, therefore, much less effective.

As we discussed in Chapter 3, *variation* is the key, and is precisely why running frequent short-term contests and only an occasional longer one will be the most effective game plan.

2) Combine Short-term Contests Into Your Long-term On-going Contests.

Whenever you do implement a long-term contest, be sure to put together a game plan focusing on some shorter term quick hit contests that can be strategically placed during the course of the long-term competition. This will be necessary to help maintain TSR stimulation.

In Chapter 3, when I touched on the subject of altering the length of contests, I stated, "The key to making a long-term contest successful is to implement a collection of shorter contests within the expanded time frame of the long one."

We then looked a the **Action Auction** as an example of a long-term contest lasting from 2-3 months. And as I also mentioned earlier, the **Action Auction** is a highly effective and successful contest.

Why? The idea is good and the prizes are fun, but, the single most important element in making this contest a success is exactly what we're referring to here: implementing short-term quick hitters on a regular basis.

The first time I ran the **Action Auction** I didn't even think to run any short-term contests during the same period. I ran it for a two-month time period and the results were positive. Some feedback from TSR's included comments relating to the length of the contest: "too long," "was fun at first, but then became boring," and "great idea, but should have been shorter."

When analyzing this feedback I realized that the people liked the contest idea, but somehow I needed to do something to maintain the stimulation during the long haul. I felt that the length of the contest itself was right, so I tried it again six months later. But this time I put in a game plan implementing various short-term contests in-between.

Although the opening **Action Auction** was a success, it didn't come close to the overall impact the second one had:

Sales were up 30% over the first one!

People were more enthusiastic because of all the excitement created by the "mini contests" which helped them increase their dollar totals for the auction itself.

And while sales were up 30%, the cost for running these additional contests was nothing.

That's right . . . . *NOTHING!*

I ran the **Money Hat** and other similar contests on an every-other-week basis rewarding people with more money for the auction. The prizes didn't change, so the cost didn't change! The TSR's simply had more simulated cash to bid on the prizes on auction day.

The employee feedback in favor of **Action Auction #2** over the initial one was resounding. Every TSR **Action Auction** since has included a game plan for integrating the short-term contests into the time frame of the long one.

The **Action Auction** is only one example. Yet, in my discussions with colleagues across our continent, this theory of frequent, short-term contests is echoed over and over again as the most effective game plan for contest success.

3) Management Leadership and Involvement Adds to Success.

As we discussed in Chapter 4, management involvement can play a major role in the success of any contest in any telemarketing environment.

Involvement by managers shows commitment, and, consequently creates additional energy in your TSR's.

Let's first define involvement. Creating the contest and then just announcing it *is not* involvement.

According to Webster "involved" means "concerned in." Synonyms for involvement from your thesaurus will show words like *commitment, association* and *interest* among others.

Do words like *commitment, interest,* and *association* describe only creating and announcing a contest? Not even closely!

How do you expect your TSR's to take interest in a contest if they don't see an interested example in you?

I guarantee it won't happen.

They must see commitment from managers for maximum effectiveness. Not that a contest won't work OK without management involvement; they can and they do.

But, is "OK" the outcome you're after? Hopefully not.

What I usually hear from managers is *"commitment means time* — and time I do not have."

Wait a minute! I'm not suggesting that you have to monitor every minute and aspect of any contest .... or even close to that. I realize that is impossible.

Believe me, I know. Having managed telemarketing operations in both the business-to-consumer and business-to-business worlds, I am well aware of the "hat rack" in your office. If it is like mine, there is anywhere from 5-10 different imaginary hats that you are wearing. Free time is certainly not a luxury with most of us.

However, I am suggesting that time for some involvement in your contests should be a priority and should replace one of the spots on your hat rack. Or if need be, you may need to add a hook!

I further recommend that when you absolutely do not have time to be involved in a contest .... *DON'T RUN ONE.* Wait until you have the time.

Certainly, this will vary depending on your position and availability of supervisors to monitor a contest.

After the initial stages of developing my department at Diebold — even without a subordinate supervisor — I was able to make the time to effectively implement contests and be heavily involved. But, as the department exploded in growth both in personnel and responsibilities, it became impossible during this time for me to be there enough to be (what I consider) effectively involved with contests.

I was either out of the office or away from the department trying to put my arms around this mushrooming growth that we were experiencing. I tried to continue to implement a few contests but quickly realized that without me there to physically lead the contests with answers to questions, cheers, recognition and necessary adjustments, the enthusiasm was at a minimum. And rightfully so.

Your people can't be expected to be enthusiastically committed when managers can't be . . . . or worse than that, won't be.

So, I stopped running contests until I was able to rejoin — and contribute to — the fun, excitement, and enthusiasm that occurs with good creative contests.

And, what a difference!

It's not luck and it's not coincidence that the more enthusiasm managers exhibit about contests, the more enthusiastic the reps will be.

Take the time, managers . . . . *make the time* to be truly involved . . . . answering questions, handing out awards and prizes, adjusting rules when necessary, and most of all, recognizing your people in person. It will make the difference between mediocre results and *great* results.

And don't forget to involve senior-level management whenever possible. Letters of recognition, phone calls and personal visits from executives will always be an enormous inspirational lift to your TSR's. Refer back to portions of Chapter 4 for further reminders on utilizing senior-level management for motivation.

4) Make Sure There Is Variation In Your Contests And Prizes.

Although I have repeatedly expressed the importance of this throughout the book, let's further explore this critical tip for success.

Let's look at a few reminders from previous chapters. Number one, you have many different interest levels you are trying to ignite. A variation of contest themes is your only hope of accomplishing that.

Use holidays; these specific dates will already bring natural excitement and enthusiasm to the atmosphere.

Remember to also use anniversary dates, sports events, culture, significant days honoring your city or state and any other ideas affiliated with special days.

Number two, the length of your contests needs to be varied to avoid predictability and ultimately bored attitudes due to redundancy.

Prizes also need to be varied for maximum stimulation.

No matter how creative you are and how many different contests you run, if the prize is always the same, the normal productivity increase associated with contests will decline.

In an operations review I performed while consulting for a company, I discovered they were only using dinner certificates and movie passes for prizes. They were using a lot of very unique contest ideas but allowing their creativity to end there. That's like wearing a tuxedo with tennis shoes! It must be a complete package for ultimate success. My last day there we ran a contest that had been used before but we changed the prizes. The contest revolved around their hometown pro basketball team, so we made the prize four tickets to the game, plus concession and souvenir stand certificates. We made sure that the cost was equal to the normal expenditures so there was no increase in prize value.

The increase came in enthusiasm and excitement from the TSR's. In talking with some of them prior to my departure, they noted that the difference was simply a new prize. Something different. Once again, I stress that people need variety.

You can also succeed at meeting the need for variety with minor adjustments to existing contest rules.

Take **The Money Hat** for example. Sometimes we ring the bell 15 times for winners, other days we ring it three times or eight times. It is always different, as are the prizes. Sometimes it is cash; other times candy bars, points for their catalog prizes, cans of pop, lottery tickets and the list goes on. We never run it the same way two times in a row.

The **Who, What, or Where Poster Board** is a natural for easy variation. Number one, it is a different poster every time. Then, I cover it with different size self-sticking notes and a different percentage of winning numbers behind those notes. The poster is also covered either right side up, upside down, or even sideways sometimes. No one knows which way it is until enough notes are pulled off the poster.

The more creative you are with: 1. different types of contests that, 2. last different lengths of time, 3. that reward a diverse group of winners, 4. with a variety of prizes, the more your people will enjoy where they're working, work harder at what they do, and perform at higher levels.

And, my fellow manager, what does that mean to you?

It means employees with better attitudes. Which in turn drives higher performance which creates TSR self-confidence . . . . and the cycle continues.

Ultimately the impact will mean *lower turnover!*

Sound good to you? Sure does to me!

Make variation part of your contest culture.

5) Calling Goals Must Be Achievable.

Don't let your imagination get carried away when determining what calling goals and expectations should be associated with a contest.

It is easy to do. As managers we often uncontrollably dream about the performance we would like to see from our TSR's.

And let's be honest. At times these dreams are totally unrealistic.

When you decide to implement any contest and you begin to think about what your TSR's will have to achieve to win, don't be a dreamer. Be a realist!

There's nothing wrong with expecting an increase in performance and ultimately productivity. In fact, that's exactly what should happen if all the elements are in place for a successful contest.

But let's not lose sight of reality here . . . .

Imagine the manager of a professional baseball team giving this speech to his players at the end of spring training: "Fellas, we're going to run a contest this season with a prize of one million dollars to anyone reaching the following achievements. A batting average of .400 or hitting 60 home runs."

One million dollars! What a prize! Great, right? Motivating, right? WRONG!

No one is going to hit .400. It hasn't been achieved since 1941 when the immortal Ted Williams hit .406 that year, marred by World War II which required many of the league's best players to serve overseas in the military. Not taking anything away from Williams; it was still a fantastic feat.

And 60 home runs?

Not likely at all. It has only been accomplished twice in Major League history and not likely to happen ever again.

It's easy to put up fabulous prizes when you know that no one will win. And even though we covered the following statement in Chapter 4, I think it's worth looking at and talking about one more time:

Calling goals associated with telemarketing contests need to be challenging, but also need to be undisputedly reachable.

You don't run a contest hoping no one will win.

I know of a telemarketing manager who used to develop contests with calling goals, that when reached, would reward that person with elaborate prizes. The only problem was that the goals his TSR's had to achieve to win these unbelievable prizes were almost unattainable.

Almost? Actually they were *proven* unattainable because no one ever reached them! Can you imagine that?

He ran different contests for nearly six months without any winners before he realized that his TSR's no longer even *cared* about contests.

Why would they care when they felt they couldn't possibly win?

And *felt* is the key word here, meaning *perception*. Because someone's perception is their reality.

Unfortunately, negative perception has a way of saturating any environment very quickly. When TSR's mentally label performance goals as unreachable, that perception will spread like a contagious disease throughout your telephone environment. The contest will be squelched before it really gets started, and, worse than that are the lingering long-term effects of this disease.

That impression of unrealistic, unattainable calling goals will remain embedded in TSR brains, and brought to the forefront when the next contest comes up. And even if the calling goals for that next contest *are* achievable the aura of disbelief that was created by the previously unreachable numbers lingers on.

At best, some of the TSR's may be inclined to buy into that "new contest, new goals, new chance to win" concept. But most will not.

And, this can become a vicious, ugly cycle until you can convince them by constant example that your goals to win contests are possible to reach by anyone in your office.

If you're going to implement contests in your telephone environment, remember the contests are supposed to help motivate your people to achieve company goals — not create problems.

When deciding on calling goals to be associated with any contest, create them to encourage your people to achieve. Set a precedent that your contest goals are realistic, fair, and most of all, achievable by everyone.

6) Use A Contest Mix That Promotes Individual And Team Winners.

Throughout the book we have stressed the importance of variation. When deciding on how many winners there will be in a given contest, variation, once again, plays an important role.

I learned the hard way that creating contests which reward only one person (the person who reaches the goals first) can be very counterproductive.

Let's look at a contest example and find out why.

We'll look at one of my early contest disasters from which I learned a costly lesson. First, let's identify the problems and then look at what I did to solve these issues by making some rule revisions.

I mentioned earlier that time off with pay is a huge motivator in our industry of business by phone. This is the prize I used in one of the first contests I ever implemented.

There was really no theme to the contest. I merely took our calling history to develop what *I thought* was a solid game plan for the contest. At that time we were making three different types of calls to prospects and customers: A renewal call (the customer's subscription was about to expire), a call to former subscribers (past customers who allowed their subscription to expire for whatever reason), and the inevitable new subscriber call (cold call to potential prospects).

The renewal call was by far the easiest call to succeed on, with the call to former subscribers next, and, of course, the cold call was the toughest of the three.

Keeping the relative difficulty of each call in mind, I attached appropriate calling goals to each group based on past history.

The people working on renewals needed 20 to win, the former subscriber people needed six to win, and the TSR's working on the new subscribers required only three to win. The contest was set up to reward the first individual to reach their goal by allowing them to go home for the evening at that time.

My brain must have been out on break when I put together this contest!

You see, word spreads very fast in an environment where there is competition. Everything started out fine until whispers were circulating that one individual was near her goal .... just one and one-half hours into the shift. Since most of the others were not even *close* to reaching their goals, this news brought with it a vacuum that very quickly sucked the energy and excitement out of everyone else.

Why should they continue to push hard? They weren't going to win. And so it was. The TSR that reached his/her goal first got to go home for the remainder of the evening . . . . leaving behind a room full of passionless people, who, for the most part, were just going through the motions.

What a catastrophe!

Here's how I fixed it: I made some simple rule adjustments which made a drastic difference in the success of the contest.

I left the calling goals the same for each functional group, but instead of only one person winning and getting to go home early, I announced that *anyone* reaching his/her individual goal would be able to leave at the time they got that final sale.

What a drastic difference in attitude and individual drive! When the first TSR reached his/her goal and got up to go home, there was no resentment or letdown from anyone else. Everyone was too busy trying to reach their own goal. And most of them did! The result was a win-win situation. Sales were up for the shift, so the corporation was ahead, and most of the TSR's were able to leave anywhere from 15 to 90 minutes earlier than normal.

The key difference was the fact that when the first person got to go home early (or the second or third), the contest was not over. Everyone still had a chance.

I also ran this same contest with slightly different rules working more as a team than individuals. I established a team goal for each functional group: renewals, former subscribers, and new subscriptions.

As groups reached their team goal, they could leave as a group. Once again the results were very positive. Each group was able to leave for the evening earlier than normal. Shift results were above normal production. Everyone wins!

I then took it one step further and put together *all* the numbers I needed, separated by functional group. I then announced that all three group totals need to be met for everyone to leave as a team.

Team effort was really displayed here! Once one functional group had reached their total, they began calling to support the other functional groups until all goals had been reached, allowing the entire office to go home early.

Whenever I talk to colleagues regarding this contest they ask with a panicky look, "You mean your entire staff left one-half hour early? What about lost production during that time?"

Well, think about it. If you prepare the contest correctly, when determining the calling goals you're going to pad your normal sales numbers by enough to cover any amount of time they miss by leaving early.

For example, if our normal production on a Monday night was 320 sales (200 renewals, 80 former readers and 40 new subscribers) I would make the goal 400 sales (250 renewals, 100 former readers and 50 new subscribers). This represented a 25% increase over the normal, so what's wrong with letting them all go when they reach this goal? Nothing. If there was no contest, true, you'd have people until the end of the shift . . . . but would you have 400 sales?

Highly unlikely!

I have used this concept equally effectively in the business-to-business world as well. Only one contest, but three different ways of winning: as an individual, a small team, or the entire staff, depending on how you set it up.

Another example would be the **Who, What, or Where Poster Board.** This creates winning for individuals, and also team possibilities each time you implement it.

As individuals reach certain goals they pull off self-sticking notes that potentially have winning numbers on them representing different prizes. As you know, the ultimate goal is to identify who, what, or where the poster is. This can be done by an individual or a team depending on how you want to set it up. Another element I have tried with success is to make the entire staff a winner if the poster is identified within a certain number of days. This way there is a total team effort while individuals are rewarded simultaneously.

Some contests lend themselves naturally to having individual winners. **The Money Hat** is very effective as a contest only rewarding one person at a time.

Run contests based on calling goals that represent an increase over each individual's normal performance. As they reach their goals they are rewarded individually.

As you develop your contests, the most effective game plan is a mixture of individual and team concept contests, with some that can potentially reward everyone. And, best of all, are contests which will possibly reward individuals, teams, and *everyone* within the same contest.

Once again, variation is a sure bet to enhance your overall plan.

7) Develop Contests That Promote "Action Attention" Among TSR's.

Action Attention is activity affiliated with a contest that takes place in front of other co-workers.

The importance of this is monumental. Not every contest has to create opportunities for Action Attention, but your contest game plan needs to include some that have this visible activity attached to it.

In Chapter 3, I referred to this activity briefly while talking about sports contests primarily. For example, TSR's shooting real baskets or putting during a contest with golf as the theme.

Action Attention feeds the appetite we all have to achieve and be recognized in front of our peers.

Take **TSR Basketball** for example. Once you reach a certain goal you get to get out of you chair and go up in front of everyone and attempt a free throw.

The *action* is the free throw, and the *attention* comes from everyone.

This is successful for several reasons. First, your teammates are cheering you on, which is highly stimulating to anyone. Secondly, your opposition is jeering or heckling you , which, in fact, is pure jealousy, or envy (or both) on their part. That is additionally stimulating. And finally, your management staff knows that you're accomplishing the goals, allowing you the opportunity for the spotlight. This should be the ultimate stimulant for any TSR.

Making or missing the shot is almost irrelevant compared to the motivation attached with just getting there and attempting the action in front of the others.

Although sports-related contests are the most obvious for creating Action Attention, most contests have some form of it already built in, or at least have the potential for it to be included.

The Money Hat, for instance, allows you to get up from your seat and strut over to your co-worker currently wearing the hat and snatch it. Everyone sees you, knows you have succeeded, and watches you take control of the potential winner. That's Action Attention in its purest form.

Same with the **Who, What, or Where Poster Board** . . . . when you successfully reach calling goals you go over and peel off a self-sticking note in front of everyone. It's Action Attention.

Some contests that I've created don't necessarily have what I call "real time" action attention, like **TSR Basketball, T.G.A. Golf, The Money Hat** or the **Who, What, or Where Poster Board.** "Real time" simply means during the actual calling shift.

I have also developed contests that promote post-shift Action Attention which can also be highly effective as motivational inspiration.

The **TSR Dart Throw** comes to my mind right away when I think about this concept. Throughout the shift, TSR's are handed raffle tickets after achieving certain calling goals. If a total team goal is reached, all TSR's with raffle tickets turn them in for chances to throw darts at a dart board after the shift is over. Each raffle ticket can be worth a dart, two darts, or whatever is decided by management. If a TSR has 10 raffle tickets and you have set the value at two darts each, that TSR gets to throw 20 darts.

The key ingredient here is the fact that someone with three raffle tickets could win over someone with ten, depending on how well the darts are thrown. Points are accumulated and winners are announced.

And all this takes place after the shift. (One additional thought here: I usually close the shift out 10 minutes early when I run this to get started with the dart throw.)

Real time or post-shift, take your pick. Better yet, mix it up. *BUT DO IT!*

Take a look at the contests you're running now as well as all the ideas coming up in Chapter 8 and see if they have opportunities for Action Attention. If they do, can it be enhanced? And if they don't, can you find a spot for some?

I hope so. Action Attention will always add that little extra that will make your contests more exciting and fun for your people, and remember, attitude drives effort.

8) Listen To Your Staff. What Motivates Them?

Your people will act on *their* motives . . . . not yours!

So, if that's true (and it is!) why don't we listen to our people more often? Or at all for that matter?

Unfortunately, many times management's ego seems to be the problem that gets in the way.

Managers, when you let this happen you might be severing the pipeline of one of your best resources for good, solid contest ideas. There is probably a gold mine of creativity within your own people, but unless *you* tap into it, it will go forever wasted.

Not only do I accept ideas from my staff, but I have run contests to receive contest ideas.

Cerainly allow your TSR's to hand in contest ideas any time, but *encourage* them to submit ideas during a structured period of time.

Let them know that for any idea that is chosen and implemented, their name will go into a drawing to be held at the end of the contest time frame. (Prizes to be determined by management.)

Try to make sure that everyone who submits a winning idea wins something. One way to accomplish this is by using the number of chosen ideas to determine how many prizes you need. Then prioritize the prizes — first to last — and allow only one winning ticket per person. So whoever wins first prize is no longer eligible to win anything else.

> **Caution here:** Those who take the time to be creative should be compensated accordingly. Therefore, I'm not so sure this is the best way to hold your drawing. If one person has submitted numerous ideas that were chosen, he/she also should have that many chances to win.

Here's a way to accomplish this: Only draw a certain number of winning tickets, with all entrants represented by as many tickets as they had winning ideas. If anyone becomes a multiple winner, great! Then, following the drawing for prizes, have some type of recognition award for those who didn't get lucky with the drawing. This way, everyone wins something. And they should.

Also, when the time comes to implement the contest for the first time, kick it off in a special way by allowing the originator to explain the contest to the rest of the people. This leadership role will create additional stimulation among your people.

Think for a moment how you would feel . . . . . .

. . . . . . your contest idea was chosen by management. It's going to be used in your office . . . . everyone else knows it's your idea and you get to announce the objective and rules to everyone else.

What's happening here? A person has achieved recognition from management in front of co-workers. Stimulating? You bet it is! And effective too. Each time I have done this, more and more ideas come in.

Talk about a win-win situation! Your people are motivated to give you contest ideas, and you end up with ideas that further stimulate them. Plus, as we mentioned in Chapter 3, you as a manager begin to identify creative people within your group.

I also recommend that you formally or informally survey your people after a contest to find out what they did and did not like about the contest idea (theme), the objective, the calling goals and the prizes.

Time and time again I speak with telemarketing managers who are blindly self-convinced that all of their people like everything about every contest they run. I hear things like "why *wouldn't* they like it," or "they *have* to like it," or even "they'd *better* like it."

These beliefs are fallacies. Here's why:

- There are a number of reasons they wouldn't like it. Were the goals ridiculous? Was the contest theme something they like . . . . or something *you* like? How about the prizes? Were they something that your people even wanted to win? Without thinking of these things in advance, there are many reasons they wouldn't like it.

● Why do they "have" to like it? Assuming that something is better than nothing, or any contest is better than no contest can set yourself up for unfortunate consequences. I've seen the following occur many times: A contest doesn't go so well due to an unpopular theme, unrealistic calling goals, a predetermined winner, unforseen circumstances, or any other reason making some of your people depressed, disappointed, angry or even bitter. You're better off not running contests at all than to wrongly assume that your people have to like every contest.

● The management attitude that says "they'd better like this contest" is the most egregious error of all. Did I miss some new legislation somewhere? Is there a new law that says when a telemarketing manager creates a new contest that everyone better like it! Or what happens then? Or else? Or else *what?* Usually when this attitude is displayed, people rebel against it just to rebel against it! Think about it. When someone tries to shove something down your throat demanding that you like it, chances are you won't. Why? Because so often when something is forced on us our human nature is to react defensively and not even give it a chance to work.

And believe me, fellow manager, our people are much smarter than we sometimes give them credit for. They will see, smell, hear or feel that "have to like it," or "better like it" attitude if it exists. If you are looking to demotivate your people, this is one of the quickest ways to succeed.

At the same time, I am *not* suggesting that your TSR's control decisions that are made regarding your telemarketing environment.

Don't misunderstand *input* to mean *decisions.*

You and your staff of supervisors must always be in control of your environment. But, employee input can be enormously valuable if you allow it to happen. And contest ideas are a great area to encourage this employee input.

And once you get that input, listen to it, and act on it when it is applicable. It makes good sense.

9) Keep Contests Simple.

Remember that nightmare I re-lived in Chapter 4 about the contest with so many confusing rules that no one even understood it? Unfortunately I think it's a nightmare that managers actually live all too often.

And I'm not sure why. Perhaps the answer is very simple.

Recently I was working with a company developing compensation and motivational game plans for their telemarketing center. As we began to look at existing contests and incentives, I couldn't believe how complicated they were. In fact, I was somewhat embarrassed because I had to have portions of it explained to me numerous times before I actually understood it.

Later on, while speaking with some of the TSR's, I learned that I was not alone in my inability to quickly grasp some of the contests' objectives.

When we began to dissect the contests further, I expressed my confusion and initial misunderstandings. I then asked the managers why the rules and goals to each contest were so complicated.

> "When we first put them together they weren't like this; we thought they were *too simple.*"

Then they further explained their reasoning; they felt that more *variables* meant more *creative.*

It is certainly a misconception that in order to create a well-developed contest you need voluminous amounts of rules and goals. That couldn't be further from reality. The simpler, the better — for everyone.

As we burrowed further into their contests, I pointed out all the work for management in preparing the contests, explaining the contest rules, *re-explaining* the contest rules, answering questions about the contest, supervising the contest, and the mind-numbing amount of tracking necessary to figure out who wins the contest.

Believe me, this grabbed their attention! Your contests need to be as simple as possible for *you* as well as the TSR's.

Whenever you initially develop a contest, and you feel that it's ready to implement, look at it one more time and see if anything can be simplified without diminishing the overall impact.

When I personally do this for all the different contests I create, more times than not I find something I can eliminate without wounding the contest. So, keep the K.I.S.S. principle in mind when developing your contests.

10) Add Props, Gags, And Gimmicks For Authenticity.

In Chapter 4, we briefly touched on how important it is to create the authentic atmosphere for your contests. Let's look deeper into this powerful tool for contest success.

Creating the authentic atmosphere for a contest will help the contest itself somehow be more believable, or better yet, more realistic.

And the more realistic it is, the more motivated your people will be about it.

Let's use Christmas to illustrate this point. You walk in a retail store after Thanksgiving, and Christmas decorations are either up, or in the process of going up. The store is covered with holiday-related materials and the sound system amplifies Nat King Cole's beautiful version of *The Christmas Song*.

What happens?

Tell the truth now . . . . a lot of you probably do what I do. You start whistling along with the music, soaking in the atmosphere as you're surrounded by decorations, slowly working yourself into the Christmas spirit!

We are *helped* into the mood by the atmosphere created. Conversely, how many people hum along to *Jingle Bells* in July?

No way! But when the decorations are carted down from the attic and your Christmas tree goes up . . . . BOOM! . . . . you're in the festive spirit.

The atmosphere has a great deal to do with it. And, so it is with contests in your telemarketing environment.

And one of the greatest advantages of doing this is the cost. Nominal fees and a little imagination go along way in setting this authentic atmosphere for any contest.

In 1986 I decided to run a contest on Halloween but hadn't put much thought into preparation for the contest. So there were few — if any — Halloween decorations throughout the office.

The contest produced fair results at best. And the thing I noticed most was the lack of enthusiasm and excitement in the air during the course of the evening.

The following year I ran a similar contest on Halloween, but prepared for it with appropriate decorations, employee costume-related prizes and other Halloween paraphernalia. There was so much more excitement in the air and enthusiasm among the TSR's.

Oh, by the way, the production numbers were up 25% over the previous Halloween.

A surprise? Shouldn't be. Upbeat, positive people usually produce better numbers, and a festive atmosphere drives a more positive attitude.

It's a beautiful and productive cycle.

No matter what theme you are using for a contest, there are easy and inexpensive ways to develop the authentic atmosphere.

In Chapter 4, I referred to my 50's-60's contest, and some easy ways to enhance it with inexpensive props and decorations. Another example that comes to mind is the **Hawaiian Beach Day** I ran in 1987 and a few other times since the inaugural event. I added some coconuts and pineapples, large surfing-related cutouts (once again purchased at a novelty store) and encouraged my people to dress accordingly.

And did they ever! A rainbow of Hawaiian shirts, "clamdigger" pants, leis, sunglasses, and even noses lathered with white zinc oxide. Accented with music from Jan and Dean and the Beach Boys, it was instant success.

I think it's the feelings that authentic surroundings create. The more the staff *lives* the contest, and bathes in it with all of their senses, the more they will respond. And the level of response will determine the success of the contest.

And this is another perfect opportunity for us to remind ourselves that this is a business that needs fun injected from time to time. If you use your imagination and take a small amount of time to be creative with props, gags, and gimmicks, the authentic atmosphere will be in place and you will be pumping in that much-needed fun.

The Eleventh Point
Although it didn't make the **Top 10,** here is another thought to help make your contests more successful, and your overall atmosphere more positive:

You must be prepared to make contest revisions in case of unforseen circumstances.

Sometimes you'll need to make changes in the calling goals, the contest rules, the length of the contest, or anything affiliated.

And if you're not on top of your contest you might not recognize this need . . . . which can and will cause internal problems.

Recently our department at Diebold began a large project calling universities and colleges across the nation to determine potential needs for electronic security products. To kick off this highly visible project, I created a contest whereby my TSR's would work toward a fictional college degree by completing these surveys. For each one completed, they received a credit hour toward their degree. Each "student" needed to complete a total of 400 surveys, so I broke it into a "Four-year program," at 100 credit hours per year. The first one to get finished with their freshman year received a small prize, as did the first person completing two years and three years, as well as the person who graduated first.

Then everyone who got their "Four-year degree" went into a drawing for a weekend at a local hotel near Ohio State University.

Everyone was giving it that ol' college try, and the "semester" was running smoothly . . . . until word came down to me that we didn't need as many surveys as originally planned.

Therefore, I should readjust the totals needed by the TSR's right?

OF COURSE!

If I don't, how fair would this be? Not very.

I immediately met with my people, readjusted their goals according to my new direction and continued on.

When a change in mission happens — which it will at times, count on it — your people will be waiting for you to react on behalf of them. And you should. You must.

Had I not been on top of that contest and made those rule revisions, my peoples' attitudes would have plummeted through the floor. And rightfully so! (We talked earlier about goals that are unattainable and how that deflates the attitudes of your people.)

Be ready. Proactively look at potential problems or situations that could arise. If they do, how will you react? What will you do?

Other circumstances will happen without warning, and you need to be ready to react to these quickly and fairly.

Although I'm sure there are other important tips for success, this chapter brings out the main ones that I feel will make the significant difference in successful or unsuccessful contests in any and all telephone environments.

7. Avoiding Post-Contest Letdown

Post-contest letdown is a genuine concern for managers and supervisors in any telemarketing environment. Whether you are in a business-to-business, business-to-consumer, inbound, outbound, corporate, service agency . . . . or any other telephone-realted atmosphere, your professionals will be stricken with this letdown.

It is inevitable. As every contest you run ends, your employees are on an immediate crash course with post-contest blues.

Whenever I speak at telemarketing conferences, or I am involved in consulting for different companies, I always hear concerns like, "What about when the contest ends? Our TSR's usually have less productive weeks following a contest." Or "How can we keep our people motivated after a contest ends?" The one I most often hear is "Our TSR's always blame their lower productivity following a contest on burnout from pushing so hard during a contest."

Are these concerns legitimate? You bet they are!

Think about it. If your contest is well-constructed, it will certainly fill the environment with excitement and enthusiasm which in turn energizes your people beyond normal. Isn't it true when people are having fun their energy seems endless? And in contrast, when you're not enthusiastic or having fun, your energy level seems to diminish rapidly or be nonexistent to begin with.

Like most people I'm certainly guilty of this . . . .

For instance, I am not a morning person at all. That's putting it mildly. Thinking back to my younger days at home, I can remember my father always needing to use two or three escalating voice tones to rouse me out of bed on school mornings. The same difficulty holds true today when that alarm blares at 5:45 a.m. to get ready for work.

But how strange! If someone calls me and wants to play golf at 6:30 a.m., suddenly it is easy to wake up, bounce out of bed, and happily glide through my morning routine. Why? Enthusiasm. Looking forward to something fun and exciting.

My wife, Kathy, often catches me dragging or grousing about too much walking in the mall after only a short amount of time shopping. She rightfully points out that there is never complaining about walking 18 holes of golf over four-to-five hours while toting a golf bag full of iron over my shoulder!

It's normal that we all posess higher energy levels when we're enthused about an activity (or *anticipation* of that activity).

Dealing With TSR Burnout

So, is it legitimate when TSR's complain to be somewhat burned out following a contest because of pushing additionally hard during the course of the actual competition?

Absolutely.

But, does legitimate mean *acceptable*? Not necessarily.

I would bet if you back up one contest with another, that post-contest letdown would not exist following the first contest. But, how long can continuous contests go on? How long *should* they go on?

I guess for as long as you can create contests, and, have the budget for them.

In Chapter 3, we looked at contest timing and some of the negative effects of constant contests. We talked about contests becoming an expectation rather than an added benefit, and all the ramifications of this attitude. An unenthusiastic lack of appreciation was one, which results in diminishing performance, and, ultimately, spells trouble. Contests must be positioned by you — and viewed by them — as a special event, and not run constantly even if you have the budget dollars allocated for this purpose.

Which brings us back to our original concern: how do we keep our TSR's up, enthused, and for our sake, productive, after a contest is over, or in between contests?

It is a question that I initially looked at in my first year with *USA Today*. But I didn't even think about this legitimate concern until it practically clobbered me over the head. I always thought that employees would be so appreciative of me running a contest that their positive attitudes and enthusiasm would simply spill over into non contest periods, and their performance would not slip from peak levels.

Come on Dave . . . .

. . . . . how unrealistic can you be?

As I look back on those early days, I cringe at how naive I was at times. Human nature is difficult to offset. And, it is human nature to be somewhat down following an extraordinarily exciting time.

You've experienced it. Think about vacations. Recall the difference between the atmosphere in the car during the drive to your vacation destination and the atmosphere in the car during the drive home. The contrast is usually staggering. On the way there the air is buzzing with natural excitement and enthusiasm. And on the way home? Normally a very quiet and subdued environment . . . . maybe even slight depression sets in . . . . as everyone reflects on the vacation that is history, and the reality that lies immediately ahead . . . . back to work, school, cold weather, or anything that is a potential "downer" compared to vacation.

Normal?

Of course. It is natural to have this letdown.

Our question, then, isn't how can we fight nature and make sure our people don't have a letdown. We can't win that fight. Don't frustrate yourself trying. They *will* go through a letdown. Instead, we need to be asking "How can we *minimize* that letdown by offsetting those inevitable blues and have production remain at very positive levels?" And one of the most important things we need to accept here is that very rarely — if at all — can post-contest productivity numbers ever equal that which takes place during a contest.

So,

> . . . . *don't equate post contest performance goals with those that are achieved during a contest.*

If you do, you will be disappointed because it won't happen often.

But be careful. That doesn't mean that these productivity numbers are necessarily bad, or even unacceptable. They might be very *good* numbers. But remember, you are comparing them to numbers which are typically higher than usual because they were produced during a period of maximum stimulation. It's like expecting a track star who broke a world record during the euphoria of Olympic competition to perform at that same speed every day of his/her regular work outs.

And if you begin to demand this inflated contest performance on an every day basis, you could be on a crash course with trouble. Let some painful experience help steer you away from the headaches I suffered in the past.

Remember earlier when I said I thought that my employees' appreciation would drive the post-contest numbers to an equal level with those that took place during a contest? And how unrealistic that was?

Well, I furthered my problems by then letting my people know that I expected that contest production to take place all the time, "now that I knew what they were capable of."

What a mistake!

Again, we sometimes do not give our people enough credit for creativity.

During the time prior to realizing the error in my unrealistic demands, my people began to hold back and stash away additional sales from during a contest . . . . to hand in *after* the contest was over. In general, the offenders were the people who realized late into the shift that they probably couldn't win, but didn't want to add to their problems by creating high expectations for increased sales numbers. So, they would conveniently tuck these sales away and not tally them so they could use them later to pump up post-contest numbers.

I know . . . . you might be thinking, "So what? What does it matter if they turn it in two or three days later? An order is an order, right?"

Only somewhat right.

Yes, an order is an order. But, the longer you wait, the longer your customer waits for that order. Is it fair to *them* for you to hold on to that order for personal gain? Certainly not.

And, when you hide an order, chances of losing the physical order form increase. I've seen it happen two different ways.

How "Held Back" Orders Can Mean Disaster

Twice I have had TSR's sheepishly approach me after having lost an order form they were holding. It was worse than trying to find a mistake while balancing your checkbook, as we had to try and go back to the actual calling list from that date and try to figure out by memory who they had sold, and then cross-check that against submitted sold forms. Once we found it; the other time we didn't.

Also, numerous times I have seen sales orders or leads change hands without consent. Let me get my paint brush out here and put together an ugly picture for you:

Usually during calling activities, reps talk to one another about individual successes. This is very normal as most people like to stroke themselves about success. So, on breaks or during lunch, words circulate, and everyone basically knows who is doing well and who's struggling.

They also find out who's "holding and hiding" orders for another time. Can you guess what's coming?

I thought I had seen it all, but apparently not. People started stealing orders from one another. Can you believe it? Actually rewriting them on new forms and resubmitting them. The TSR's who lost these orders were afraid to say anything to management because they knew they probably faced trouble for holding and hiding, plus they couldn't always remember the contact information on the form. So as one-hundred to three-hundred orders were getting processed days later, the stolen orders just became mixed in with the bunch.

Terrible situation! (With obvious personnel integrity problems beyond the stolen orders you'd need an entire other book to deal with.) Keep in mind these paper-type operations were performed manually. I realize that automated coputer environments limit or erase altogether some of these situations.

Another problem that arises when reps are holding orders is incorrect daily productivity numbers resulting from wrongly filled out tally sheets: tally sheets that TSR's forgot to change when they decided to hold that particular order or orders.

In the early days at *USA Today* we were not automated at all. At the end of each shift we had to manually tally up every rep's hours, calls, and sales. The totals of these sheets (and there were usually anywhere between 100 to 200 tally sheets per shift) had to equal the number of physical orders we had handed in. So, if someone held onto an order but marked it on their tally sheet, the numbers wouldn't match. So, as a management team we would have to go back and recount the orders and cross-check all the tally sheets hoping to find our error. The problem was, it wasn't *our* error. Many times we went through hours of number crunching trying to find a mistake that didn't exist. What a nightmare! The only way to solve it was to break down tally sheets and physical orders by rep and find the discrepancy. Hours and hours of hair-pulling, hand-wringing aggravation.

These are just examples of problems that arise when TSR's hold and hide orders, leads, appointments or whatever your call type.

And so began my quest to find an answer to the post-contest blues, which were becoming an epidemic after most contests. After making the decision to not run contest after contest, and learning the hard way that demanding or expecting productivity equal to contest-time performance was unrealistic and counterproductive, I can remember feeling like there was no answer in sight.

And then, as it does so many times, the answer came somewhat by accident. Following a four-day contest affiliated with the **Who, What, or Where Poster Board** the post-contest letdown began to cloud the atmosphere as it usually does. And then one of the TSR's fired the final piercing arrow . . . .

   "Are we going to have some type of contest tomorrow?"

And with that I finally snapped. (Internally only, of course.)

I started thinking to myself about peoples' expectations of me and anything related to their job, and I began cooking from the inside out like I was in a microwave oven.

How could these people expect another contest *already?*

Easy. They knew ol' Dave would have another one brewing right around the corner. There always was. No matter what happened in between, contests were not usually too far apart, so they were smug in their belief that another one was qued up all ready to go.

This thought process (even though it was true and I knew it) fried me even more.

In fact, as so often happens when we feel we're being taken for granted, I began thinking a bit irrationally..... questioning myself and the number of contests I did run for them. Why *should I* run another one so soon? Why should I *ever* run another one?

The more I thought about this, the more I worked myself into a lather as to why they didn't deserve it. Contests had gone from being a luxury . . . . a special event . . . . to an unappreciated expectation.

"Well I'll fix them," I thought as I reclined in my chair with my arms cossed and a sinister grin on my face, "I won't run any contests at all. We'll see how they like **that!**"

I was all ready to carry out this potentially suicidal plan . . . . when I began to reclaim my common sense. It struck me like a lightening bolt. The idea that rescued me from the depths of despair. And it seemed so simple. Why hadn't I thought of it before?

The people will have to earn the next contest.

That's it! It's that simple.

As I first thought about it, it *seemed* that simple. Later I would find it to be initially more difficult than anticipated, but in the long run, it has been the most successful formula to increase numbers in off-contest times while positively impacting the atmosphere simultaneously.

OK, great, you're saying, but why does it work and how do you do it?

"Why" is very simple. Your people want contests. They want the competition and they want the rewards.

Making them earn the next contest adds a couple of other important factors: achievement, and recognition for that achievement.

In earlier chapters we talked about the fact that all of us want to achieve and we all starve for recognition. Using this formula of earning the next contest forces the achievement to gain the recognition: another contest.

However, the first time I used this idea it did not go over very well. Keep in mind that my people were so used to having contests that the events were expected and not appreciated. So when I announced that the next contest would have to be earned, it was not well-received. In fact, it took days before the reality of it seemed to sink in.

And with that reality came some defensiveness, some withdrawal, and even some anger from the employees. Consequently, by spending so much energy on negative reactions they didn't have enough left to reach their goals and earn the right to another contest.

And that's when I made the worst blunder you could possibly imagine at this point:

I went ahead and gave my people the next contest even though they had not earned it.

What a regretful mistake!

It is my opinion that there are only remote cases that correctly fit Leo Durocher's quote, "Nice guys finish last." And, unfortunately, this was one of those remote cases. Trust me . . . . don't do what I did. For one good reason: when this mistake is made you *add* to the very TSR expectation problems you are trying to avoid.

Here I was trying to make sure my people got away from expecting contests and what do I do? Give them one when they haven't reached the goals I set for them to earn it!

The result of my error was that the next time I set goals for them to reach in order to earn the following contest, they were nodding in mock agreement, thinking, "Yeah, right Dave."

They assumed I would give it to them anyway. But when they didn't reach the goals and I didn't give them a contest, they felt scorned.

Nothing but bad things can happen when you make this mistake. So don't make it.

When you set goals for your TSR's to earn a contest, make sure you walk your talk. If they earn it, they get it. If they don't, they don't. It's that simple.

I only made this mistake once. Not only did my people gradually come to accept the challenge of earning the next contest, but they understood it.

Your reps' appreciation for contests will increase dramatically when they periodically have to earn them. The appreciation naturally comes from the accomplishment.

Implementing Post-Contest Letdown Insurance

How to implement this is equally as simple as why it works. When a contest is finished, do the number crunching necessary to figure out how much your productivity increased during the course of the contest.

You might be asking yourself "Increased over what?" If so, the answer is,

increased over your normal performance numbers.

Your history should show you what those numbers are, and you should know them.

In the telemarketing environments that I have managed I have always kept close records manually — or on a PC — that track productivity by hour, shift, day, week, and month. By doing this I have always been able to more accurately forecast upcoming performance based on this history. When you calculate what your increase has been you are ready to put together a solid plan for your staff to earn the next contest.

Again, when setting your goals, don't be a dreamer! Take your normal performance averages and your live contest numbers and come up with a compromise somewhere in between: numbers that reflect an increase over normal but that take the post-contest drain of your TSR's into account.

Keep in mind that these post-contest times are not really that at all! You have a contest without really running one.

Make sense? Sure it does. The contest is to reach certain goals to earn the next real contest. These are goals to win a reward, so *it is indeed* a contest.

If you are in a telemarketing environment where your TSR's are performing the same function day in and day out, it is easier to forecast what production numbers should be.

When I managed a regional telemarketing center for *USA Today* our function didn't change. Every day was another day to sell newspaper subscriptions by renewal to former subscribers or to those that had not yet subscribed. So, in between any contests it was a cakewalk to forecast what production should be. I knew what lists we would be calling, what normal performance was like on any given day of the week, what calls-per-hour should be, and what the closing percentage should average. Everything is based on a continuous history.

Now, however, it is very difficult in the corporate culture of a business-to-business environment where my TSR's are responsible for very different calling functions and could be working one market research or sales project during a contest but a very different calling campaign in post-contest times. Different script lengths and project objectives are two of the variables making it extremely difficult to decide what calling goals should be to earn the next contests. For example, my people may be working lead generation during a contest. Just prior to the end of the contest I get new direction involving a market research project that must get completed. This project has a script length that is much different from lead generation; completing a survey is easier than generating a lead and the decision maker is more difficult to reach. How do you take the numbers from the contest period to calculate contest earning goals? Obviously you can't. You need to look back on projects that might have some similarities to the new one, or, if that fails you may have to use your experience and expertise to pick arbitrary goals that should be reached.

I have had to perform this "dart throw" many times. The one key here is to remember to be flexible. In the previous chapter revealing 10 Tips For Successful Contests, we closed by emphasizing the need to be prepared to make contest revisions. We have to realize that when our TSR's get on the phone with new projects, our guess work based on all our experience and knowledge, coupled with role play sessions, is just that . . . . guess work. Be ready to make adjustments.

Whether you are business-to-business or business-to-consumer, inbound or outbound, service agency or corporate in-house, large or small, manual or automated, your people will suffer post-contest letdown. But, regardless of your telemarketing application, you can calculate a formula to implement in between contests. Will you take the time to do it? The fact is you *must* do this to minimize that letdown in order to maximize performance, and, ultimately, profits.

You can't eliminate this letdown. It will exist. What you can do is accept it, deal with it, and offset it by making your people earn the right to another contest.

8. 79 Contests That Work

As you reference this chapter of contest ideas from around the globe, it is important to remember some of the highlights from our journey through the previous chapters.

Not all contests will work in every environment. There are too many variables: size of staff, age of people, inbound or outbound, business to business or business to consumer application, corporate or service bureau . . . . and the list goes on.

You need to be flexible and creative simultaneously.

These contest ideas that make up this chapter are innovative, but, most of all, they are successful. Each and every one has "tested positive" in the telephone environment where they were created. Some have also been used around the country and prove to be equally successful in other telephone centers.

I have received both written and verbal proof that **"The Money Hat"** and **"The Who, What, or Where Poster"** are widely used and highly effective in many telephone environments nationwide. Sometimes used just as they are and other times they have been slightly modified.

That's the key! Flexibility. Looking at these ideas with an open mind as opportunities for your own atmosphere.

Each time you look at one I encourage you to ask yourself, "Is this feasible for my area?", or "Could this fit our application with a few moderate changes?", or even, "Could this work for us as is?"

Once you answer *yes*, the next question is simple: "How?"

If you like the concept, or feel it could be successful with your people, work with it. Twist it, bend it, revamp it, and mold it to fit your area. Let your imagination run wild!

While initially preparing this chapter I identified numerous contest ideas that I can't wait to use in my area right away. Some of them require only slight revisions, and that makes my job easier. And, I'm convinced I will uncover more each time I turn to this chapter.

I'm sure you will share in my excitement as you begin selecting from the contest ideas that currently help create and maintain a positive and stimulating atmosphere in telephone environments around the world.

Have fun!

1. 50's/60's

Contest Creator: Dave Worman

Title: Manager of Corporate Telemarketing

Company: Diebold, Incorporated

Location: Canton, OH

Contest Description: A 1950-1960 era-related contest where reps earn 50 or 60 points by reaching calling goals throughout the day, and answering era-related trivia questions. Bonus points for best dressed, and knowing your music and your points could turn into potential dollars or prizes. Try it, you'll have a really "Boss" time!

Material/Supplies Needed:

- 1950's/60's office props

- 50's/60's trivia questions

- Simulated cash

Contest Goal: Have a "Blast From The Past" while increasing sales numbers.

Duration: One day or shift.

Contest Rules/Guidelines:

- Everyone dresses accordingly in 50's/60's related clothes and hair styles.

- For reaching preset productivity goals a TSR earns 50 points (use simulated cash).

(1. 50's/60's continued)

Contest Rules Guidelines *(continued):*

- With each 50 points comes a trivia question from the 50's/60's (correct answer doubles your points).

- Spontaneous bonus questions asked throughout the day.

- At break, judge 50's/60's outfits and award three prizes: 1st-110 points (50 + 60); 2nd-60 points; 3rd-50 points.

- TSR's with top three point totals at end of day win.

Special Tips For Success: Put together a promotional flyer prior to contest. Call a radio station to play 3 hits for your office at break time. Anyone correctly guessing the song title and artist wins additional points.

This contest always generates enthusiasm starting with precontest anticipation through the end of that day. Lots of fun. Production numbers have always increased a minimum of 10%.
Dave Worman

2. Grab Bag

Contest Creator: Helen Day

Title: Call Power Manager

Company: Ohio Bell

Location: Cleveland,Ohio

Contest Description: Reps earn the right to select a grab bag of goodies after reaching calling goals.

Material/Supplies Needed: Sample-size consumer product items, such as mouthwash, toothpaste, hairspray, soap, etc. (Items costing less than $1.00).

Contest Goal: Our goal was to increase the sale of add-on services.   For example, we were at 94% of our cross-selling and up-selling objective. We went up to 120% to 130% of objective as a result of the contest.

Duration: One week.

Contest Rules/Guidelines: Each supervisor prepares a large sack of grab bags for their group. The way we ran it was when Customer Service Reps sold 10 of a certain product, they earned the right to go into the grab bag and picked out a mystery gift.

Special Tips for Success: Buy different colored bags or decorate brown paper bags, and buy a large variety of useful items.

Contest was successful because it was short and everyone was interested in what others were receiving. No one wanted to be left without a bag.   Helen Day

3. Bingo

Contest Creator: Teri Maas

Title: District Manager, Line Advertising

Company: PennySaver

Location: Vista, CA

Contest Description: Keep your sales reps focused on achieving their goals while playing **Bingo**. Reps earn the right to fill spots on their **Bingo** cards by reaching call objectives listed on the cards. TSR's will realize immediate gratification, but the difficulty to get **Bingo** increases throughout the contest. This will escalate your peoples' performance while enhancing their telephone skills.

Material/Supplies Needed:

- Prepare a **Bingo** card with 15-20 different call objectives. You'll want to repeat a few on the card, as you'll be filling 25 squares.

- Six cash incentives weekly.

Contest Goal: To fill **Bingo** card by achieving all goals, either horizontally, vertically, or diagonally each week.

Duration: Flexible . . . . . six weeks has worked well for us.

Contest Rules/Guidelines:

- Pick 15-20 common sales objectives, tasks and goals you want your people to focus on.

(3. Bingo, continued)

Contest Rules/Guidelines *(continued)*:

- Sales reps fill in spaces by completing tasks. Manager can initial square upon verification.

- Department manager selects direction to focus on that week. Sales rep gets cash bonus for each line they complete. There are several options the department manager can use to select the direction: any horizontal line; any vertical line; any diagonal line.

- Each of the B-I-N-G-O letters (For example, "B" across & "B" down for the first week, "I" across and down for the second week, etc.).

Special Tips For Success:

- Vary degree of difficulty for tasks so some are achieved quickly, but there is a least one on each line that will be a challenge.

- Have cash available to pay on the spot!

This provides excellent motivation for tasks employees are expected to do regularly. It applies to any department, whether sales or support, and keeps the energy level high. It's a lot of fun! Teri Maas

4.Travel

Contest Creator: Philip Cohen

Title: Telemarketing Consultant

Company: Philip Cohen Consultant AB

Location: Skelleftea, Sweden

Contest Description: Reps work toward the major prize, which is a trip to a destination you choose. The excitement comes in following individuals' or teams' progress toward the destination on a map as production goals are met by your people.   First one to reach the destination wins and enjoys the trip.

Material/Supplies Needed:

- Map showing office location and a destination, which will be the prize if targets are met (For example if your company was located in Miami, and goals reached would provide the winner with a trip to Orlando, the map would show both Miami and Orlando).

- All types of tickets and vouchers (travel tickets, entrance tickets to special events, shows, restaurants).

Contest Goal: The winner (individual/all sales teams/best sales team — which you prefer is up to you) who achieves the production goal is awarded a trip. This could be an event (Super Bowl), an attraction (Disneyworld), a city (why not a trip to London?), or the head office. The main thing is that both your sales office and the winning destination can be pinpointed on the map, so that as progress is made towards the goal, this can be illustrated on the map for all to see.

(4.Travel, continued)

Duration: If the destination is expensive, the competition can be up to two-three months long. As with most contests much of the zing goes out of the air if it is too long. My experience is that it's difficult to focus on goals long enough, and often a winner becomes obvious all too early, so that perhaps four-five weeks is generally more appropriate.

Contest Rules/Guidelines: A goal is set, and as progress is reported daily it is charted on the map so that the contestants can see how far they have come towards their goal. For example, if the prize is a trip to London, you can indicate on the map the route an aircraft flies from New York to London. As progress is made, a small airplane can be drawn on the map showing how far the team has traveled. As each country (or city or state) is approached, you might throw out a few travel brochures showing the next city/state/country that will be reached to keep interest from waning.

This can also be run on a smaller scale, showing a map of your city with the destination being a theater, resort, sports arena, restaurant, or other attraction. Have mid-point prizes along the way .... perhaps a gift certificate to a nice restaurant along the route for the individual or team getting there first, and also a lesser prize for those trailing, maybe something like MacDonald's or Burger King coupons.

As to rules otherwise, they are up to you. The main thing is to have an agreed goal that can be measured objectively, and that daily reporting is made in the form of progress being indicated on the map.

Special Tips for Success: See that there is a truly objective measurement, so that there are not a lot of discussions after the contest closes as to who actually won. I once saw this competition carried out in a company based in Stockholm with the goal being

(4.Travel, continued)

Special Tips for Success (*continued*):

a weekend in Amsterdam for the best sales team over a three month period. The second and third teams were so disappointed at not winning this prize that they requested a recount of the results, and then another recount! The time lost in doing recounts, and the resulting animosity, severely clouded the benefit of increased sales that the contest had generated. Ideally, there should be a prize that everyone can win; even the lowest-performing salesperson can win a Big Mac. Be careful not to make the prize too large. I saw the same company that had a trip to Amsterdam one year, offer a trip to London the next year; the third year the prize was a trip to USA, and then it had all escalated so much that when the following year's contest was announced, a trip to Helsinki, the sales teams regarded it as a snub that they had been degraded with such a lowly prize; they expected at least Hawaii!!

Special Bonus: In Europe, where I live, the tax man is always trying to find ways of taxing prizes. This competition has the added bonus that it can be adapted to the tax situation; it is always possible to justify a reason for a trip to *somewhere* to study the competition/local conditions/a foreign partner, therefore being an attractive way of giving a prize without creating more tax for the winner.

Excellent way of visualizing the goal, and showing progress towards it other than with mere figures. And life can be kept in the contest for a fairly long time if the supervisor keeps coming up with travel brochures, or the menu from the next restaurant on the map.
Philip Cohen

5. Let's Make A Deal

Contest Creator: Janet Meyer

Title: TeleSales Manager

Company: Harris Publishing Company

Location: Twinsburg, Ohio

Contest Description: Modeled after the zany TV game show, **Let's Make a Deal**, your reps are awarded boxes or envelopes and can trade for others before opening their prize. Fun and excitement will fill the air while sales become the grand prize, with management the winner.

Material/Supplies Needed:

- Sign and/or hat that says "Monty" on it for manager to wear (Monty Hall from the game show **Let's Make a Deal**).

- Three large, three medium, and three small boxes.

- Envelopes and other interesting containers marked A,B,C, 1,2,3, etc. Use brightly colored envelopes, especially if some are green, to make the contest more interesting.

- Fake money.

- Money-sized paper with sayings such as "Have a great day!" written on them.

- Various prizes to fit your budget, including free lunch vouchers, savings bonds, gift certificates, and cash money (which should be in the form of ones, fives and tens, with

(5. Let's Make A Deal, continued)

Material/Supplies Needed *(continued)*:

the amount of each denomination dependent upon your budget).

Contest Goal: For our contest, the goal was to quickly attack leads and close sales on a specific campaign.

Duration: This contest was run for one month, with the game being played each week.

Contest Rules/Guidelines: Each TSR was given an equal amount of leads for a specific campaign. They were told the object of the contest, and the rules: For every three leads closed on this campaign, the TSR would get a chance to play **Let's Make a Deal**. Each player gets a choice between three boxes, three envelopes or any combination they wanted to put together of three boxes or envelopes. Before they open it, they get a chance to keep it or trade it for whatever you (Monty) offered, such as another envelope or box, or the money in your hand (five ones fanned out in a hand is very appealing), or a crisp five dollar bill. Also give them the opportunity to trade among the other players, if each party is willing. Be sure to add "Zonk" prizes like the "Have a nice day!" cards.

Special Tips For Success: Have fun with it! The more zany you are in being Monty, the more fun the TSR's will have. Be sure to determine what your realistic goals are beforehand.

We closed that campaign in record time with a higher close ratio than on any previous TeleSales campaign. In addition to that, the TSR's had great time playing the game. They were able to quickly hit the leads while they were hot, and were rewarded with some fun when they closed the sales.   Janet Meyer

6. Gumball Contest

Contest Creator: Susan McConnell

Title: Director of Sales

Company: South Hills Data Comm

Location: Pittsburg, PA

Contest Description: TSR's earn gumballs each time they meet a productivity goal. But they don't chew them . . . . they store them until the end of the contest when the dollar values are announced for the various colors. This builds the excitement and enhances the productivity until the very end.

Material/Supplies Needed:

- Gumball machine
- Certain number of colored gumballs, the number of which will be determined by what dollar value you want to assign to each (for example, 25 blue gumballs worth $10 each, 50 red at $5, and so on)
- A glass jar for each rep to store and display their gumballs

Contest Goal: Encourage strong productivity.

Duration: Two to four weeks.

Contest Rules/Guidelines:

- Each time a goal is achieved, let reps turn the crank for one gumball.

(6. Gumball Contest, continued)

Contest Rules/Guidelines *(continued):*

- Each Rep keeps gumballs earned in glass jar on their desk for the duration of contest.

- At the end of the contest, announce the cash values of the colors. Everybody wins, since those with most gumballs do not necessarily get the most cash, as some luck is involved. Depending on budget available, the value of each color is up to you.

This promotion has consistently raised productivity by 15% on outbound calling. Susan McConnell

7. Square Deal (or Four Square)

Contest Creator: Mary Ann Bodanza

Title: Sales Supervisor

Company: Revere Products

Location: Solon, Ohio

Contest Description: Each time a rep reaches your performance goals, they are able to select a numbered square on the master board of 56 squares. When the board is completed, squares are uncovered with prizes awarded to the achievers.

Material/Supplies Needed: Poster board with 56 squares, numbered 1-56.

Contest Goal: Our goal was to increase number of daily orders and introduce product lines.

Duration: Approximately three weeks.

Contest Rules/Guidelines: The prizes corresponding to the numbered squares are in a sealed envelope. TSR's who reach your goal for the day go up and write their name in a blank square. For example, we used four orders earning one square, eight orders earning two squares, etc. After all 56 squares are filled, special prizes are revealed. Our prize values were as follows: one square = $100.00; one square = $50.00; 34 squares = $5.00; 20 squares = two hours off (maximum of four hours off at one time). Hours off at discretion of supervisor.

Gives TSR's chance to compete with fun while at the same time increasing sale productivity.   Mary Ann Bodanza

8. The Money Hat

Contest Creator: Dave Worman

Title: Manager of Corporate Telemarketing

Company: Diebold, Incorporated

Location: Canton, Ohio

Contest Description: As reps reach calling goals, they earn the right to take possession of the coveted **Money Hat**. If they have it on when the bell rings, they win the prize.

Material/Supplies Needed:

- Hat

- Simulated currency

- Table top bell

Contest Goal: To increase TSR productivity.

Duration: One day or shift.

Contest Rules/Guidelines: Tape dollar bills on the hat using monopoly money or other simulated currency. Management then predetermines calling goals which are announced to the people, and numerous bell ringing times which are left undisclosed. When the shift begins, the first TSR to make a sale, appointment, lead, etc., gets the honor of wearing **The Money Hat**. The next person to meet a predetermined call goal is able to saunter over and snatch **The Money Hat**. The cycle continues. Management rings the bell at each of the undisclosed, preset times. Whoever has the hat on when the bell rings wins cash.

(8. The Money Hat, continued)

Special Tips For Success: Fifteen rings a shift could be worth $1.00 each, or five rings at $3.00 each, or even three rings at $5.00 each. Associate fewer rings with higher rewards and scale it accordingly.

One of the most popular contests I've ever created. People love to take the hat from their co-workers. Dave Worman

9. The Winner Is . . . .

Contest Creator: Diana DiRobbio

Title: National Telemarketing Manager

Company: Colony Communications, Incorporated

Location: Providence, New York

Contest Description: A delayed reaction contest. Managers determine what the "secret goal" will be for that evening, write it down, and then place in a sealed envelope. The next day before the shift begins, the manager opens the envelope to reveal the goal from the previous day. Whoever achieved that goal gets to pop a balloon containing a strip of paper explaining the corresponding prize.

Material/Supplies Needed:

- Balloons

- Strips of paper

- Envelope

Contest Goal: To increase sales/hours; to decrease absenteeism and tardiness.

Duration: No time limit.

Contest Rules/Guidelines:

- Write out your prizes (monetary or otherwise) on strips of paper, put in balloons, and hang them around the room.

(9. The Winner Is . . . . , continued)

Contest Rules/Guidelines *(continued)*:

- Write "The Winner Is . . . ." in **BOLD** letters on the envelope and place where all can see it (preferably manager's/supervisor's desk). Each shift manager/supervisor will write on a piece of paper what will determine that shift's winner. For example, "The rep who gets the most sales," or "The rep who made the first sale after break," "The rep who has perfect attendance for the week," and so on. The paper is then folded and placed in the envelope and sealed. Only the manager/supervisor knows what is written. The next night before reps get on the phone, the manager/supervisor opens the envelope and reveals what is written, saying, "The winner is . . . ." The winner gets to select a balloon, pops it, and reads what is written on the strip of paper (the award/prize). Reps love it!

Special Tips For Success: Give everyone a chance to win even though they may not be the top rep sales- or volume-wise.

Everyone knows they can be a winner! Diana DiRobbio

10. Dead Celebrities

Contest Creator: John Anderson

Title: Program Manager

Company: Direct Telemarketing Services

Location: Hudson, Ohio

Contest Description: Reaching your goals enables your TSR's to exhume a celebrity (actually just their name) from the coffin box, while trying to remember their claim to fame in order to earn a prize.

Material/Supplies Needed:

- Coffin Box

- Slips of paper with **Dead Celebrities'** names on them.

Contest Goal: Increase sales and give much needed positive reinforcement from management.

Duration: Daily.

Contest Rules/Guidelines: Slips of paper with names of dead celebrities are put in a box resembling a coffin. Every time an order is made the manager goes to the TSR work station with the coffin and lets the TSR pull a slip out of the box. If the TSR identifies that person's claim to fame, they receive a bonus. Then for an extra bonus the TSR has to identify the cause of death. This contest works great because the TSR wants to participate and it lets you as a manager acknowledge their sale by saying something positive to them. I find the amount of money is not important; it's the praise they look for. To the outside observer this game sounds

(10. Dead Celebrities, continued)

Contest Rules/Guidelines: *(continued)*

really morbid, but all the TSR's love it! In fact, when a celebrity dies, reps call in and tell us to add a new name.

Special Tips For Success: Enthusiasm and sincere managerial-compliments add greatly to the increase in results.

Nothing livens up our office like Dead Celebrities. Usually we see an immediate 5-10% improvement in production as well as a significant jump in employee morale. John Anderson

11. Ring Up Sales

Contest Creator: Jillian R. Hassler

Title: Senior Account Executive

Company: Direct Telemarketing Services

Location: Hudson, Ohio

Contest Description: Each time reps produce a sale or lead, they ring a small bell, which alerts the supervisor to update that rep's sales on the department tote board. Callers earn the right to ring a larger bell — in front of everyone — when reaching a major goal. TSR visibility and managerial recognition highlight this performance booster.

Material/Supplies Needed:

- Small bell for each work station

- One large bell for manager's desk

Contest Goal: For the reps it's to ring the large bell more times than anyone else in two weeks-one month period. For you as a manager the goal is to increase production in the targeted areas, such as leads, sales, appointments, etc.

Duration: Ongoing for small bells, one month for large bell contest.

Contest Rules/Guidelines: Each time the TSR gets a lead, sale, etc., they ring the small bell on their desk so the supervisor can mark it on a dry erase board. When the TSR reaches his/her quota they get out of their seat and ring the large (louder) bell in the middle of the room. This immediate recognition is motivational in creating a positive, competitive work environment.

(11. Ring Up Sales, continued)

Special Tips For Success: Verbally recognize each bell as well as noting it on a visible board. Also you can doubly reward the "ringers" with prizes for both the small and large rings.

Ringing a bell at the close of each sale brings immediate recognition and praise for a job well done. Focusing on the positive helps motivate employees to strive for achievement.   Jillian R. Hassler

12. Dialing for Dollar$

Contest Creator: Sylvia Alvarez

Title: Telephone Sales Operations Manager

Company: JC Penney Life

Location: Plano, Texas

Contest Description: TSR's buy letters of the alphabet with phoney dollars earned for beating production goals set by management. The letters then are used to help solve word puzzles.

Material/Supplies Needed:

- Phoney dollars

- Unit boards with stick on letters

- Department puzzle card and individual puzzle cards.

Contest Goal: To help increase awareness of production goals, and progress toward achievement of the annual plan. Also, to help foster a team selling approach while matching recognition to budgeted production goals.

Duration: One year.

Contest Rules/Guidelines: Individuals who meet or beat production standards are awarded phoney dollars. The play money is used to buy letters of the alphabet. Each unit has a game board

(12. Dialing for Dollar$, continued)

Contest Rules/Guidelines *(continued)*:

on which letters are posted next to the players' names. The better the players' production is, the more phoney dollars they win and the more letters that can be purchased for posting. A giant puzzle card is posted in the department, and each week clue letters are filled in on the department card. Individuals or groups meeting their goals are allowed to guess the puzzle on the puzzle board. At the end of play, prizes are awarded at an annual banquet based upon the number of letters collected. And, groups who guess the puzzle are recognized for their achievement, and win incentive gifts.

Special Tips For Success: Phoney dollars and puzzle clues should be given out weekly. Letters can be purchased, puzzles will be solved, and incentive gifts should be awarded monthly. Larger parties are suggested each quarter, and a banquet should be held with major prizes awarded at the end of the year. Something can (and should) be going on all the time. This keeps the staff involved and interested and contributing to the success of the program.

Dialing for Dollars was both motivating and fun for the Telephone Sales Representatives. They worked hard to meet the sales goals in order to win prizes and they checked the puzzle board every day hoping to be the first in their unit to solve the puzzle. Sylvia Alvarez

13. Wheel of Fortune

Contest Creator: Dave Worman

Title: Manager of Corporate Telemarketing

Company: Diebold, Incorporated

Location: Canton, Ohio

Contest Description: TSR performance will be at a maximum as they try to solve puzzles under **Wheel of Fortune** rules. The action and intensity increases as someone knows the puzzle but must first get a sale to earn the right to solve it out loud for everyone. Prizes follow, another phrase posted, and the game begins again.

Material/Supplies Needed:

- Fortune wheel

- Large letters

- 8 1/2 x 11 cardboard pieces to post the phrases, places, things, persons, events, etc.

Contest Goal: To increase sales.

Duration: One day or shift.

Contest Rules/Guidelines: Large letter cards are posted in reverse on the side walls of the office, spelling out a phrase, place, thing, or person. For reaching goals, a TSR may choose a letter they think could help them solve the puzzle. If guessed correctly, the cardboard letter is then turned so the entire office can see the unsolved puzzle. A vowel can only be bought with a credit card order (or whatever slightly more difficult objective you choose).

(13. Wheel of Fortune, continued)

Contest Rules/Guidelines: *(continued)*

If a TSR spins and stops on a "Free Spin" they get to spin twice. When someone solves a puzzle, they can then spin the **Wheel of Fortune** and win anywhere from $1.00 to $7.50. Another puzzle is then posted and the game begins again.

Special Tips For Success: Have a female supervisor be Vanna for the day. Allow TSR with most accumulated money attempt to solve special puzzle at shift's end for grand prize. Use the TV shows rules for final puzzle.

Always generates a great deal of enthusiasm! Dave Worman

14. Top Dog Races

Contest Creator: Mark Schmidt

Title: Project Manager

Company: Ameridial, Incorporated

Location: Canton, Ohio

Contest Description: TSR's will "go to the dogs" by reaching production goals that get them into the racetrack clubhouse and earn cash to wager on their favorite puppies. Actually, the dog track is your office, where a video of the race is shown at the end of the week, or end of the contest. Everyone placing a bet on the winning dog splits the Jackpot.

Material/Supplies Needed:

- Dry erase board

- Raffle tickets

- VHS recorder

- A tape of a dog race. This can be obtained by taping a race if you have a TV (or cable) channel that rebroadcasts races.

Contest Goal: To increase sales while creating excitement in the center.

Duration: One week

Contest Rules/Guidelines: Reaching production goals first gains admission to the "track." Definitely make sure everyone can at

(14. Top Dog Races, continued)

Contest Rules/Guidelines: *(continued)*

least reach this level. Reaching further goals buys a ticket to bet on the dog race. Bets are placed daily on the dog of their choice. For each bet placed, money accumulates in the jackpot. All players betting on the winning dog will split the jackpot. If no bets were placed on the winning dog number, the jackpot rolls over to the next race. Races on video will be run on Fridays or upon completion of the project. Show and place (2nd and 3rd) winners' names will be held for a special drawing at the end of the races.

Special Tips For Success: Create the authentic atmosphere. For example, create a program and come up with names for the dogs, perhaps names that have some silly relevance to the department (or managers' names). This can also be adapted to horse races.

This contest has done more to create excitement and a high increase in productivity than any I've ever created. Mark Schmidt

15. Buried Treasure

Contest Creator: Matthew Yates

Title: Sales Manager

Company: Video Arts

Location: Chicago, Illinois

Contest Description: As TSR's reach calling goals they're able to visit a giant poster or picture and go on a treasure hunt. They earn stickers which they place on spots where they believe the "buried treasure" is located. At week's end you announce the predetermined locations, and the closest stickers to them represent contest winners.

Material/Supplies Needed:

- Large piece of paper on which you'll create your "map," or a poster or actual map of some area.

- Small sticky labels.

Contest Goal: To motivate sales staff. To find the buried treasure location.

Duration: One week or more.

Contest Rules/Guidelines: Draw a tropical island with trees, huts, lagoons, caves, etc. (or football field/baseball field/golf course) on a large piece of paper. Or, use a poster or map. Select a number of various spots on this piece of paper but DO NOT mark the paper. Allocate a prize to each spot you've chosen. Vary the prize size. Every time a rep meets certain criteria they take a small sticker and initial it and place it on the paper. At the end of the

(15. Buried Treasure, continued)

Contest Rules/Guidelines: *(continued)*

week, the people whose stickers are nearest each selected spot win that prize.

Special Tips For Success: Be creative in the design of the island, etc. Do the prize unveiling with everyone present in the meeting.

The contest provided the group with a common focal point and topic for discussion. Friendly competition between reps resulted which generated increased activity in a fun environment. Matthew Yates

16. Park Place Walk of Fame

Contest Creator: Sandra Borchers, Jane Burch, Anne-Marie Peterson

Titles: Inbound Acct Rep, Nat'l. Acct. Rep, Outbound Acct. Rep

Company: Travelodge

Location: Mission, KS

Contest Description: A long term contest loosely modeled after the Monopoly board game. Reps earn the right to roll the dice and move around the game board, shooting for weekly awards and the ultimate annual grand prize.

Material/Supplies Needed: Poster board, metal rim name tags (their playing pieces) with velcro back, fastened to velcro on outside of game board.

Contest Goal: To challenge an individual's personal productivity and promote teamwork.

Duration: One year, with awards given weekly

Contest Rules/Guidelines: Design a gameboard like Monopoly's, with prizes or points replacing the properties. Players must reach specific goals, such as contacts, conversion, revenue, etc., in order to roll one die. Perfect attendance allows them to roll two dice. Each week the goals are higher than the week before (very small increases). When they land on a prize, they win it! Players begin with a green name tag to mark their spot on the board. After exceeding certain levels, the player earns a different colored name tag which then awards them double or triple in value. Special bonuses are given for high levels of call quality. As players pass "Go" they collect 200 points. The clerical workers

(16. Park Place Walk of Fame, continued)

Contest Rules/Guidelines *(continued):*

participate when the department exceeds the weekly goal. At the end of a year, the person with the most points receives the grand prize.

Special Tips For Success: Because the Incentive/Recognition Program was developed by the participants, they are continually analyzing and promoting the program within each work group. Recognition and awards should be done on Monday to set the tone for the week. Competition is against oneself and everyone encourages each other. Increases in goals should be obtainable.

17. Call For a Free Lunch

Contest Creator: Merritt Mattson

Title: Executive Vice President

Company: Consumer Preferred

Location: DePere, Wisconsin

Contest Description: This contest will work best in a consumer telemarketing environment where a straight script is followed. Make your new TSR's believers in your system while letting them earn a free lunch. During initial calling, new TSR's are able to reach your goals and receive $10.00 and ring the alarm signifying a successful sale. This contest helps them get started on a positive note.

Material/Supplies Needed:

- Three $10 bills

- Telechart (script)

- List of prospects

Contest Goal: To help new telemarketers gain confidence in their ability to perform the job.

Duration: Normally about a half hour.

Contest Rules/Guidelines: In our situation, a group of people are placed in a phone room, given a telechart (script), and a list of prospects to call and establish an appointment. The first three callers who get an appointment receive a $10.00 prize. A new group then enters the room and we repeat the process.

(17. Call For a Free Lunch, continued)

Special Tips For Success: Ring an alarm every time someone gets an appointment or sale.

The synergism created by the competition for the monetary awards made the phone calls fun rather than drudgery.   Merritt Mattson

18. TSR Poker

Contest Creator: Dave Worman

Title: Manager of Corporate Telemarketing

Company: Diebold, Incorporated

Location: Canton, Ohio

Contest Description: Deal your people some escalated performance goals and watch them have fun building the best poker hand. Single playing cards are awarded as goals are reached by reps, who then work to continue building their hand. Watch the poker faces surface! Best hand at the end of the contest wins the pot.

Material/Supplies Needed: Two or three decks of cards

Contest Goal: To create room energy and increase sales.

Duration: One-three days

Contest Rules/Guidelines: Tape the playing cards on a wall or pin them to a bulletin board face down. For reaching production goals, TSR's choose cards one by one until contest time frame is over. Best hand wins.

Special Tips For Success: Have smaller prizes for anyone having drawn a certain amount of cards.

Everyone loves the thrill of turning over face-down cards. People keep their poker hands to themselves until the contest ends, which adds to the excitement. Dave Worman

19. Silent Contest

Contest Creator: Deborah Aebly

Title: Insurance Counselor

Company: Economy Premier Assurance Company:

Location: Freeport, Illinois

Contest Description: You'll keep your people in suspense, and performance up at the same time by making your calling goals and contest time frame a secret until after the contest is over. Reps are never sure if a contest is actually on, and what might be measured, so all areas of performance remain high.

Material/Supplies Needed: Gift certificate, or other prizes.

Contest Goal: To reward the employee who puts forth that extra effort every day, not just at contest times.

Duration: One week.

Contest Rules/Guidelines: This is a silent contest, so it is not mentioned until after the contest is held. You should randomly choose one week out of any month and one every day job function of your employees which can be tracked and totalled. For example, ours was most applications received per individual for that specific week. At the end of the month, after the figures have been calculated, the contest should *then* be announced and the employee with the highest statistics is presented with the gift certificate.

You may be surprised to see a little more of that extra effort every day at your work place as no one knows when the next silent contest may occur.   Deborah Aebly

20. Quota Busters

Contest Creator: Thomas J. Winn

Title: Telemarketing Manager

Company: Solvay Animal Health

Location: Mendota Heights, MN

Contest Description: TSR's achieving specific product quotas receive points which could equal prizes. This equation builds excitement over the contest period. And as quotas are met, so are company revenue goals.

Material/Supplies Needed: None.

Contest Goal: Motivate telesales staff to achieve quota on specific products.

Duration: At least a month, and generally two or three months

Contest Rules/Guidelines: Each product we sell has an individual quota, by rep. I'll pick out five or six products (generally high margin products). For each product that a telesales rep meets or exceeds a monthly quota, they are awarded one point. If the contest runs for two months, and contains six products, the reps can earn a total of 12 points. I usually will award a bonus of one point per month if any rep would meet or exceed quota in *all* the products. Person with the highest point total at the end of the program wins. Prizes have been cash, dinner for two, or time off with pay. Try to award a first and second place prize. What's great about this contest is that as people achieve their quotas, the department and company revenue goals are met. Everyone wins.

(20. Quota Busters, continued)

Special Tips For Success: Sometimes management picks the products in the contests, and sometimes the reps themselves do the honors. It has been very successful so far.

This contest is always a win-win situation. The telesales reps win as their commissions are based on margin dollars sold. The higher the margin, the more commission earned. Should they win the contest, they win again. The company also wins as more high margin products are sold. This increases the bottom line. Thus we have a WIN-WIN-WIN SITUATION. Thomas J. Winn

21. The Dollars Per Hour Challenge

Contest Creator: Curt Herwers

Title: Supervisor of Telesales

Company: Bankers Systems

Location: St. Cloud, MN

Contest Description: Regardless of sales style, this contest can be won by any TSR. Their total revenue generated is averaged out for your contest time frame, therefore rewarding those with the highest dollars per hour ratio. Reward anyone reaching your goal, or the highest two or three percentages.

Material/Supplies Needed: Tally sheet or software that measures time on phone, along with sales statistics.

Contest Goal: Motivate all reps at once, despite various sales styles.

Duration: As short as one hour, as long as one year.

Contest Rules/Guidelines: Every rep is an individual. Some make long phone calls and deal with many objections. Others move quickly and play the numbers game more effectively. The key to evaluating performance is what dollar amount per hour of actual work, or phone time, they achieve. There are a couple of different ways to reward winners: 1. Announce that whoever can attain (X) dollars per hour of selling over (X) period, wins (X) prize. 2. Award tiered performance levels (A) baseline, (B) achiever, (C) overachiever. This helps everyone aspire to baseline, but continues to incent high rollers to drive onward.

(21. The Dollars Per
Hour Challenge, continued)

Special Tips For Success: Educate your TSR's on statistics, such as dollars per hour, dollars per call, conversion (close ratio to contracts), etc. The more they graphically understand that every potential order affects their day/week/year, the more energy and commitment and effort they'll give it.

Each TSR, regardless of specialty, will learn to see a way to include themselves in this contest. Your "objection resolution specialist" will go the extra mile to make the sale. Your "speed dialer" will focus even harder on what each deal means to performance. And all TSR's will remember to cross-sell, because every contact resulting in dollars puts them in the money. It's a lot of fun. Try it hourly, daily or weekly! Curt Herwers

22. Journey To The Moon

Contest Creator: Dave Worman

Title: Manager of Corporate Telemarketing

Company: Diebold, Incorporated

Location: Canton, Ohio

Contest Description: Add fuel to the motivational fire of your TSR's with **Journey to the Moon**. Reaching calling goals equals fuel necessary to make the trip to the moon. Additional fuel (performance) is needed to safely land. Watch for malfunctions! Who will make the moonwalk?

Material/Supplies Needed: Outer space and astronaut-related props and pictures.

Contest Goal: To increase TSR productivity.

Duration: One day or shift.

Contest Rules/Guidelines: Break your TSR's into teams of astronauts. Reaching calling goals (sales, appointments, leads, etc.) equals fuel, which moves the team's craft into positions to land on the moon. Bonus fuel is awarded for any orders with anniversary-related criteria. This includes addresses/names/phone numbers that include *Neil, walk, moon, 720, 1969, space, or Armstrong*. Malfunctions caused by incorrectly filled out orders, incomplete phone presentations, etc., will delay safe landing. Additional sales, appointments and leads are needed to land. The first (any) team of astronauts to land safely wins the award(s). Astronauts providing the most fuel for each team make a moon walk and receive an additional prize.

(22. Journey To The Moon, continued)

Special Tips For Success: Use theme-related prizes. (I used tickets to the movie Spaceballs and free tanning at Moonglow Tanning Spa).

Run this close to the anniversary of Neil Armstrong's Moonwalk (7/20/69) and your results will take off! Dave Worman

23. Employee of the Month

Contest Creator: Gene A. Lupi

Title: Inbound/Outbound Telemarketing Manager

Company: I. C. S.

Location: Scranton, PA

Contest Description: Performance, attitude, quality and dedication will make a TSR Employee of the Month. This contest will energize your TSR's to get their name in lights each month.

Material/Supplies Needed:

- Small cork board

- Employee photos

Contest Goal: An employee is chosen from the ranks of our Inbound and Outbound Telemarketing departments, and from support personnel as the top employee of the month.

Duration: New contest each month.

Contest Rules/Guidelines: The following criteria are used to select the winner each month: 1) Overall performance: meeting or exceeding quotas, goals, paperwork and housekeeping responsibilities. 2) Attitude: must show excellent attitude toward the company, products, department and co-workers. Must show the ability to work well with supervisors and monitors. 3) Dependability: ability to follow instructions, good attendance and reports to work on time able to meet responsibilities and with a minimum of supervision. 4) Quality: will go the extra mile to do a good job for the department, company and customers.

(23. Employee of the Month, continued)

Special Tips For Success: Make the prize worth working for. We give a $40.00 gift certificate to a local restaurant chosen by the winner, plus two movie tickets, and a reserved parking space for one month.

The Employee of the Month program is really open to all employees because it narrows the individuals' performance qualification to a particular month and does not take prior performance into consideration. Morale and expectations for the program are generally high. Gene Lupi

24. Envelope Pass

Contest Creator: Dave Worman

Title: Manager of Corporate Telemarketing

Company: Diebold, Incorporated

Location: Canton, Ohio

Contest Description: Reaching calling goals will gain immediate ownership of one of the two sealed envelopes that pass throughout the room as sales are made by everyone. But, only one has a prize; the other one is empty. TSR's may choose which envelope they want as each sale is made. At day's end, envelopes are opened by current owners and a prize is won.

Material/Supplies Needed: Two envelopes.

Contest Goal: To increase sales.

Duration: One day or shift.

Contest Rules/Guidelines: One envelope has "Prize," or "Bonus" written on slip of folded paper. The second envelope has a blank sheet of folded paper. When a TSR makes a sale (designate a minimum dollar amount to qualify), she/he chooses one of the envelopes, but does not open it! When the next sale in the room occurs, the TSR either takes the envelope from the other TSR, or substitutes the envelope sitting on the manager's desk. If that same TSR makes the next sale, she/he has possession of both envelopes. When a TSR makes the next sale, he/she will choose an envelope from the TSR. At the end of the night, the TSR's left with the envelopes open them to see who has the winning envelope.

(24. Envelope Pass, continued)

Special Tips For Success: Attach helium balloons to the envelopes so everyone knows who has them.

Works best with mid-to-large sized staffs.   Dave Worman

25. The Phone Power 600

Contest Creator: Jim Domanski

Title: Communication Manager

Company: Telecom Canada - Phone Power

Location: Ottawa, Ontario, Canada

Contest Description: Short-term rewards and pit stops highlight this car race-themed contest. Team or individual competition will successfully enhance performance and visibly show progress.

Material/Supplies Needed:

- Two clotheslines

- 300 clothespins

Contest Goal: Our goal was to achieve 600 leads by year end (Hence The Phone Power 600).

Duration: Two months.

Contest Rules/Guidelines: The contest was designed for both individual and team motivation. Two teams are created to create a competitive, race car environment. Each group has a clothesline and 150 pins. Every time a TSR gets two leads he/she would go to the clothesline and remove a pin. (The pin is saved by that particular TSR). The point was to visually see your team goal being met and to have individual interaction. There were three phases: 1) The first team to take off 50 clothespins (i.e., 100 leads) would win. 2) Phase II was another 50, and, 3) Phase III was the same. (This represented short-term, attainable goals) Hourly awards of $10.00 gift certificates were made in Phase I; in Phase

(25. The Phone Power 600 continued)

Contest Rules Guidelines *(continued)*

II, the gift certificates are $20.00 and Phase III, $30.00. Contest should feature Pit Stop lunches, pizza, etc.

Special Tips For Success: Encourage full participation by teams and individuals; have them cut out road signs, string the clothesline, organize the pit stop, etc. Have some very nice awards every now and then.

The Phone Power 600 enabled us to visualize our progress individually and as a team. While the rookie TSR's would take off their clothespins one by one, the veteran would strategically wait until the opposing team had a comfortable lead before removing them from the clothesline. This contest really increased the competitive spirit and generated some good natured fun. Mark Ward, Veteran Telemarketer

26. Ticket Draw

Contest Creator: Linda Sanvido

Title: Telemarketing Manager

Company: UZ Engineered Products

Location: Cleveland, Ohio

Contest Description: Simple and effective! A roll of raffle tickets and some padded performance goals are all you need for fun and success. As goals are reached, tickets are awarded and everyone gets ready for the drawing.

Material/Supplies Needed: Roll of duplicated ticket coupons.

Contest Goal: To earn as many tickets as possible, thereby increasing the chances of having a ticket drawn.

Duration: Two week period.

Contest Rules/Guidelines: Tickets are based on the following schedule, which shows the dollar amount of the order, and the number of tickets earned for that order:

$100/1 ticket
$200/2 tickets
$300/3 tickets
$400/4 tickets
$500-1000/5 tickets
$1000 and over/7 tickets

(26. Ticket Draw, continued)

Contest Rules/Guidelines: *(continued)*

At the end of the two-week period, a ticket is drawn and the person holding the ticket is the winner. This is the type of contest that, due to the luck of the draw, makes it workable in a mix of veteran salespeople and rookies.

Contest will increase sales volume and the number of orders. Rookies and veterans alike get excited and have a chance with this contest. Linda Sanvido

27. Points

Contest Creator: Cecilia C. Dorsey

Title: Sales Manager

Company: Pulsar Industries, Incorporated

Location: Cleveland, Ohio

Contest Description: Sales reps earn points which are awarded based on types and levels of sales. The person with the most points at the end of the contest period wins the prize.

Material/Supplies Needed: Prizes (We use two tickets to a comedy club, dinner and cocktails).

Contest Goal: To get the most points.

Duration: One week.

Contest Rules/Guidelines: Here's how we run it: Each order must be over $50.00 to qualify. Points are awarded as follows, 1) All new customers, five points; 2) All second or third orders, four points; 3) All orders from a customer who hasn't ordered within the past year, three points; 4) All orders over $1000.00, two points; 4) All other orders, one point. Reps can only get points from one point category per order. The person with the most points wins the contest.

Special Tips For Success: Concentrate on getting new customers!

Free food, drinks and a show for a sales rep and guest was a terrific prize. Everyone went for the new account points. We all love competition and winning. It was a busy week. Cecilia Dorsey

28. Who, What, Or Where Poster Board

Contest Creator: Dave Worman

Title: Manager of Corporate Telemarketing

Company: Diebold, Incorporated

Location: Canton, Ohio

Contest Description: Each time a rep meets a goal, he/she earns the right to visit the **Who, What, or Where Poster Board** and remove one of the self-sticking notes, therefore revealing more of the poster. Reps receive prizes for the notes, and for guessing who, what, or where the poster is. Inexpensive and highly effective!

Material/Supplies Needed:

- Poster

- Self sticking notes

Contest Goal: To increase sales productivity while solving the mystery of **Who, What or Where.**

Duration: One-seven days

Contest Rules/Guidelines: Purchase a poster of a celebrity, famous place, or an object, and cover it with straight lines of very small self-sticking notes. Then put the poster board up in the most visible part of your center. Establish calling goals and announce them to your TSR's the day of the contest. As TSR's reach your goals, they go up and pull off a note to reveal a small portion of the poster. This continues until someone thinks they can identify who, what or where the poster is. If the TSR is correct, a prize of your determination, and the poster, is awarded

(28.Who, What, Or Where Poster Board, continued)

Contest Rules/Guidelines: *(continued)*

to that TSR. If incorrect, the contest continues until the poster is successfully identified. Depending on the size of your staff or the size of the poster, this contest can last up to seven days.

Special Tips For Success: A TSR must have a certain amount of self-sticking notes to make a guess. (Log each person's pulls.) Associate 25 to 40 percent of the notes with smaller awards, such as time off, extra breaks, cash, extra pulls and others. Write numbers on the back of the 25 to 40 percent of the notes and keep a master list of what awards those numbers represent. Use large posters and do not always cover them right side up (turn sideways or upside-down prior to covering with self-sticking notes).

Always a winner, especially when it takes days to figure out what direction the poster is in. Dave Worman

29. Spring Into Summer

Contest Creator: Terri Joski

Title: Sales Support Supervisor

Company: West Publishing Company:

Location: St. Paul, MN

Contest Description: Help motivate your TSR's during the beautiful summer months when everyone would rather be outside. Similar to Contest 19, **The Silent Contest**, weekly productivity goals are held secret, and each week a winner is announced after the fact. Everyone must concentrate on every aspect of performance to possibly win.

Material/Supplies Needed: Variety of fun summer-oriented prizes: lawn chairs, BBQ grills, car care sets, beach towels, walkman, fishing pole, golfing items, pool or water gear, etc.

Contest Goal: Our goal was to increase sales productivity in all areas: lead generation, highest outgoing sales, most outgoing dials, best lead generation story, all within a small budget.

Duration: 12 weeks.

Contest Rules/Guidelines: Each week there is a prize winner based on what management chooses as the goal for the week: most leads generated for field representatives, highest outgoing dials, highest outgoing sales in general or of a specific publication, best lead generation story told in a group meeting, etc. The goal is not announced, so the sales staff is never sure in which area to concentrate. This motivates them to increase productivity in all areas. The winner was announced at the end of the week based on statistics.

(29. Spring Into Summer, continued)

Special Tips For Success: Keep it fun and simple. Our Sales Associates would walk by the display of prizes each day and discuss what they would like to win.

The Spring Into Summer sales contest really was fun! It rejuvenated our Sales Associates and motivated them in their daily calling. The great thing about this contest is Sales Associates remember it and continue to bring it up as a sales contest they enjoyed and would like to see happen again.   Terri Joski

30. Let's Go Fishing

Contest Creator: Joanne B. Dawson

Title: President

Company: JBD Enterprises, Incorporated

Location: Wauconda, Illinois

Contest Description: TSR's reaching your calling goals get to go fishing by pulling paper fish replicas out of a large glass fish bowl or tank. Some will be winners . . . . and others won't, and must be tossed back in. When the special grand prize fish is caught, it represents 1/2 day off.

Material/Supplies Needed:

- Glass fish bowl

- Construction paper

Contest Goal: Without spending money, to keep reps motivated during the summer, because it's difficult to sit inside on the telephone when it is beautiful outside,

Duration: Summer months

Contest Rules/Guidelines: Make construction paper fish and put them in a big glass fishbowl. Every time the reps make a sale, they get to go fishing. A good prize is time off, which doesn't cost any actual money and is tied in with being able to be outside, instead of sitting at the telephone on a beautiful day. Prizes we've used are: take an extra hour for lunch, come in tomorrow at 10 a.m., or go home an hour early. The biggest fish (or grand prize) was to take the afternoon off to GO FISHING.

(30. Let's Go Fishing, continued)

Special Tips For Success: We made it a contest that everyone won—some more times than others—and everyone received a prize.

Fishing is synonymous with summer, a time when it is very difficult to sit at a workstation and make phone call after phone call. So, because this contest was held during the summer, it not only increased sales, but it also improved morale and spirits.
Joanne B. Dawson

31. Pictionary

Contest Creator: Mary Ann Bodanza

Title: Sales Supervisor

Company: Revere Products

Location: Solon, Ohio

Contest Description: Turn this popular game board idea into additional profits in your telephone environment. Teams of TSR's that reach calling goals will play for prizes at the end of the contest. Pictionary rules apply, making this a very popular chance for visibility and fun.

Material/Supplies Needed:

- Pictionary deck of cards

- Easel or blackboard

- Markers and timer

Contest Goal: Increase sales, develop team spirit and have fun!

Duration: 10 working days

Contest Rules/Guidelines: Divide department into teams of four or five players. 1) Team chooses own artist. 2) Opposing team chooses category. 3) Artist draws from pictionary deck and has 30 seconds to begin drawing. 4) Team has one minute to guess picture. 5) Teams that tie with the most right answers will have a playoff. 6) Winning team will be the one with the fastest right answer in the playoff. 7) Set team goals, such as sales, dollars per hour, etc. 8) Only qualifying teams play. 9) Whole department shuts down for 15-20 minutes to watch.

(31. Pictionary, continued)

Special Tips For Success: Be prepared to laugh!

Try this because win or lose, everyone wins. It is a real favorite here at Revere, for we have played it many times. Mary Ann Bodanza

32. TSR Football

Contest Creator: Dave Worman

Title: Manager of Corporate Telemarketing

Company: Diebold, Incorporated

Location: Canton, Ohio

Contest Description: Two teams square off against each other, and by reaching calling goals, gain offensive yardage toward touchdowns. Allowing TSR's to dress in team colors, and posting a scoreboard visible to all will help enhance the atmosphere. Watch out for penalties, and award an MVP!

Material/Supplies Needed: Football props for office.

Contest Goal: To increase TSR productivity and promote team effort.

Duration: One day or shift.

Contest Rules/Guidelines: Divide the shift/day into halves, with break time/lunch time representing half time. As TSR's reach calling goals, they produce offensive yardage toward touchdowns worth seven points each. Two penalties (incorrectly filled out orders, incomplete presentations, etc.) on either team rewards the opposing team a field goal (three points). The highest scoring team at shift's end is the winner and is awarded pizza the following week. The MVP (most offensive yardage on either team) is awarded a trophy.

Special Tips For Success: Use a cap gun to end the first half, and the game. Use yellow penalty flags (made from simple yellow

(32. TSR Football, continued)

Contest Rules/Guidelines: *(continued)*

fabric). Have management, supervisors or verifiers wear referee shirts and use whistles appropriately. If possible, award the MVP with tickets to the actual game.

Announce the game in advance and people will dress for the occasion and come ready to play! Always drives production up.
Dave Worman

33. TSR Football (Another way to play)

Contest Creator: Dave Worman

Title: Manager of Corporate Telemarketing

Company: Diebold, Incorporated

Location: Canton,OH

Contest Description: This concept keeps your entire staff working together as the home team against the clock. Interchanging on offense and defense, the clock can stop the TSR team from scoring, or score on its own if you don't play solid defense.

Material/Supplies Needed:

- Clock

- Football props for office

Contest Goal: Increase performance. For the entire office to team up and beat their opposition, the clock.

Duration: One day or shift.

Contest Rules/Guidelines: Your entire staff is the Home Team. The clock is the Opposing Team. You might want to simulate an actual big game involving your local pro or college team. Announce the upcoming game two weeks in advance to allow time for staff to dress accordingly (Jerseys, T-shirts, buttons, etc. of Home Team.) Divide shift/day into first and second halves. (A break or lunch can signify halftime). TSR's alternate offense/defense every half hour. While on offense, reaching goals against the clock earns yardage toward touchdowns. Determine how much yardage to award for each type of goal. On defense,

(33. TSR Football-
Another Way to Play, continued)

Contest Rules/Guidelines: *(continued)*

their job is to prevent the oppositon from scoring. They do this by meeting or beating their calling goals for the half-hour. If they fall just a little short, award the Opposing Team a field goal (three points), or for lower performance, the opposition scores a touchdown (seven points). Choose an MVP (combination of offensive/defensive contributions), and award the trophy at a "post-game locker room celebration." If the TSR Team wins, award them with pizza the following week.

Special Tips for Success: Run this contest right before the actual game you are simulating.

Promotes TEAM unity and drive. TSR team has never lost!
Dave Worman

34. Hot Potato

Contest Creator: Miriam Wolk

Title: Personnel/Training Director

Company: Dialogue Marketing

Location: Southfield, MI

Contest Description: The highest dollar sale will grab the **Hot Potato** from the previous holding TSR. This continues until shift's end when the Hot Potato turns into a prize for someone.

Material/Supplies Needed:

- Envelope with hot potato drawn on outside (Or use an actual potato, and have the envelope on the manager's desk)
- Prizes

Contest Goal: To make the highest sale possible.

Duration: Pass it around as many times as you need to do so in a four-hour shift (that's how we do it!).

Contest Rules/Guidelines: Whomever gets the highest sale, gets the potato. The person who has the potato at the end of the shift, wins whatever is inside the envelope: money, lottery tickets, movie tickets, etc.

Special Tips For Success: Hype up the balance of the people who don't have the potato. Ring a bell for whomever gets the potato.

Always an increase in daily sales!   Miriam Wolk

35. Card Elimination

Contest Creator: Linda Sanvido

Title: Telemarketing Manager

Company: UZ Engineered Products

Location: Cleveland, Ohio

Contest Description: TSR's start the contest with a hand full of playing cards. The goal is to get rid of them. To do so, after meeting goals, they pick a card from the manager's deck. If it matches one in their hand, they get rid of the card. First to get rid of all card wins, or fewest cards at contest's end wins.

Material/Supplies Needed: Two decks of playing cards, with different patterns on the backs.

Contest Goal: Pick a type of call/order you want to see instant increases in. Ours was to increase number of $100 + orders.

Duration: Two-week period

Contest Rules/Guidelines: At the onset of the contest, distribute evenly throughout the department the cards from one deck. The second deck is held by the manager. For every $100 + order, a rep selects a card from the manager's deck. If it matches one in the rep's hand, that card is eliminated along with the one from the main deck. First person to get rid of all cards wins (Or, the person with the fewest cards).

Contest will increase sales volume and the number of orders. Rookies and veterans have reacted enthusiastically over this contest.
Linda Sanvido

36. Money to Minutes

Contest Creator: Dave Worman

Title: Manager of Corporate Telemarketing

Company: Diebold, Incorporated

Location: Canton, Ohio

Contest Description: TSR's exceeding management's goals are awarded simulated dollars that turn into equivalent minutes ($50 = 50 minutes). Minutes can then be used to go home early or come in late.

Material/Supplies Needed: Monopoly money or other simulated currency.

Contest Goal: Increase sales while TSR's to go home early.

Duration: One day or shift.

Contest Rules/Guidelines: Use monopoly money or other simulated currency and decide on production goals and corresponding dollar amounts before shift begins. Any credit card sale is worth extra dollars. Any play money accumulated during the shift is cashed into the number of minutes that he/she can leave early that night/day. For example, $50 = 50 minutes. Any TSR leaving early or arriving late will also be paid for the entire shift.

Special Tips For Success: Use a special stamp on the simulated money for identification purposes. (This keeps people from bringing Monopoly money from home to add to their totals.)

Time off is a huge motivator making this a stunning success.
Dave Worman

37. Balloon Bombs Away

Contest Creator: Miriam Wolk

Title: Personnel/Training Director

Company: Dialogue Marketing

Location: Southfield, MI

Contest Description: Reaching goals will reward TSR's with darts to burst balloons after the shift. Prizes are in every balloon on small paper pieces.

Material/Supplies Needed: Balloons, darts, bulletin board, pieces of paper with prizes listed on them.

Contest Goal: To increase daily sales quota.

Duration: One daily shift

Contest Rules/Guidelines: For whatever type of sale is made, a rep earns a dart. At the end of a shift they shoot at the balloons. There are pieces of paper inside the balloons indicating a prize. Prizes include lottery tickets, movie tickets, Godiva chocolate, etc. The balloons are shot at from a marked distance.

Special Tips For Success: Walk reps by balloons individually or as a group. Tell them great prizes are listed inside; just earn a dart and burst a balloon!

Absenteeism always decreases during this contest. Miriam Wolk

38. Sales Olympics

Contest Creator: Jeannette Fannin

Title: Director, Sales and Marketing

Company: Hardware Sales Company:

Location: Cordova, TN

Contest Description: Various indoor sporting activities highlight this exciting contest. As TSR's reach specific calling goals they get to engage in different events to earn money.

Material/Supplies Needed: Indoor basketball goal and ball; child's ring toss game; indoor putting green.

Contest Goal: To earn as many turns at the games as possible, which will generate money for the TSR's.

Duration: One day or shift.

Contest Rules/Guidelines: When TSR's reach the first tier of calling goals they qualify for the "games." When they reach the next tier of performance, they get five basketball shots worth $.25 each per success; the next level earns them four ring tosses for $.50; finally, at the top tier, they get the right to sink five easy putts worth $1.75 each.

Special Tips For Success: Use your imagination here and come up with your own "Olympic events." Create the authentic atmosphere, and have gold, silver, and bronze medals for the top three money winners.

Attitude, teamwork and fun equalled ALL TIME RECORD HIGH SALES! Jeannette Fannin

39. Spring Fling

Contest Creator: Lori Bradish

Title: Inside Sales Manager

Company: Schneider Communications, Incorporated

Location: Green Bay, WI

Contest Description: TSR's earn points for successes at various milestones in the sales cycle. Points turn into time off tracked on a large flower (thus the Spring theme) with a petal representing each person.

Material/Supplies Needed: Construction paper, gold stars.

Contest Goal: To increase productivity.

Duration: One month, usually right before Memorial Day (But also easily adaptable to "Fall Frolic," "Winter Whirl," etc.).

Contest Rules/Guidelines: The way we did it was that a point system was worked out for various parts of the sales process. For example, successful introductory calls where the prospect was qualified and literature was sent was worth a certain number of points. Closed sales on second calls were worth more. Each point was equal to one minute. Each rep could accumulate up to 240 points (four hours) to be used the Friday before Memorial Day. We tracked points on a flower. Each rep had a petal and for every 15 points a gold star is put on their petal.

This not only increased sales, but also revs up activity at every phase in the process. This was also motivational for new employees.
Lori Bradish

40. The Account Manager Derby

Contest Creator: Jeannette Fannin

Title: Director, Sales and Marketing

Company: Hardware Sales Company

Location: Cordova, TN

Contest Description: They're off! TSR's must earn forward progress for their horse by reaching performance goals. Competitive spirits will visibly surface to win this race.

Material/Supplies Needed:

- Long board designed as a race track
- Wooden horses on sticks to be placed in holes along the track

Contest Goal: To reach the end of the track and collect $30.00.

Duration: One week.

Contest Rules/Guidelines: Reps must first reach certain productivity goals to enter their horse in the race. Each additional sale is worth a link down the track.

The Account Manager Derby inspired our Telephone Account Managers to race toward their sales goals! Jeannette Fannin

41. Bonus Bucks

Contest Creator: Susan McConnell

Title: Director of Sales

Company: South Hills Data Comm

Location: Pittsburg, PA

Contest Description: Based on their all-around performance, attendance, and discipline, TSR's earn Bonus Bucks. At contest's end, the top accumulators of Bucks get to use them to select prizes . . . . . some of which might even have hidden cash inside.

Material/Supplies Needed: Fake bonus bucks and various prizes.

Contest Goal: To raise productivity and meet objectives daily.

Duration: One month.

Contest Rules/Guidelines: Bucks are awarded for meeting certain productivity criteria (We change ours every day). For example, most orders for previous day, first outbound call, last order of day, first person to work . . . . etc. Rep who has earned most bucks for the month gets first choice of prizes; second highest gets second choice, etc.

Special Tips for Success: Choose prizes around a theme. Have hidden cash in some of the prizes — perhaps some of the lesser ones — to create more excitement.

This promotion raised our productivity (in terms of leads uncovered) by 25% while promoting a fun competitive atmosphere.
Susan McConnell

42. Holiday Incentive

Contest Creator: Lori Bradish

Title: Inside Sales Manager

Company: Schneider Communications, Incorporated

Location: Green Bay, WI

Contest Description: Get in the holiday spirit and help your reps earn some Christmas cash. Reaching goals allows TSR's to choose an ornament on the Christmas tree. Although each ornament has a number, not every number is a winner. Presents (prizes) are awarded for certain special numbers.

Material/Supplies Needed: Christmas tree, or someplace to hang ornaments; cash or prizes.

Contest Goal: Increase sales.

Duration: December

Contest Rules/Guidelines: We decorate a tree and attach a number to the hook of each ornament. The number is then checked against the manager's master list of prizes. Each number has potential for a cash prize (60% chance). Some ornaments don't have a prize. The rep can pick an ornament every time he/she makes a sale.

Special Tips For Success: Get a variety of ornament types.

This helped the department get over their reluctance to call prospects over the holidays. They sometimes assume that everyone will put them off till the new year. Not true! Lori Bradish

43. Pumpkin Bowl Contest

Contest Creator: Linda Weigle

Title: Inside Sales Supervisor

Company: Cleveland Cotton Products

Location: Cleveland, OH

Contest Description: A list of prizes is posted, along with corresponding goals needed to reach (cross sells, up-sells, new accounts, etc.) in order to be eligible for that prize. Achievers have their name placed in a pumpkin (or other holday-related receptacle). Winners are drawn each day for the prizes.

Material/Supplies Needed: A container like a pumpkin, Easter basket, etc. You can write their names on pumpkins cut from paper, or eggs at Easter, hearts at Valentine's Day, Christmas trees, turkeys, flags for the 4th of July, etc.

Contest Goal: Emphasis on objectives for the TSR's, and a chance at a prize for attaining each objective.

Duration: One week

Contest Rules/Guidelines: Each TSR attaining one of the objectives wins a chance at a prize of the day. I list the prizes with pictures and a list of objectives. You can choose an objective for each day or use the whole list for each day. The list could include cross-sales or up-sells; each five orders they turn in, or when they solve a customer complaint or open a new account. Each morning we stir up the pumpkins and draw a winner for the previous day's production. This kicks off the day with some added enthusiasm. Prizes can be seasonal as well.

(43. Pumpkin Bowl Contest, continued)

Special Tips For Success: It's not always the size or cost of the prize that's the incentive — it's in breaking the monotony.

Our inside sales representatives enjoy this contest because it keeps them motivated around a holiday.   Linda Weigle

44. Easter Egg Hunt

Contest Creator: Miriam Wolk

Title: Personnel/Training Director

Company: Dialogue Marketing

Location: Southfield, MI

Contest Description: Exceeding goals by a certain percentage earns TSR's the right to hunt for eggs. The more by which they exceed their goal, the higher the value of the eggs they are allowed to search for.

Material/Supplies Needed: Different colored plastic eggs.

Contest Goal: To increase sales quota, dollars, or for perfect attendance.

Duration: One week.

Contest Rules/Guidelines: If increased sales dollar quota is achieved (by at least 10%) for the week, or the rep has perfect attendance for the week, let them go on a hunt for one plastic egg of a specified color for that level. Eggs for increase of 10% over sales quota would be another color, and have a greater value prize in them than eggs for perfect attendance.

Special Tips For Success: Use a daily tally sheet that would show how much more a rep has to sell in order to search for an egg.

This contest always improves our attendance level.   Miriam Wolk

45. TSR Basketball

Contest Creator: Dave Worman

Title: Manager of Corporate Telemarketing

Company: Diebold, Incorporated

Location: Canton, Ohio

Contest Description: A team-oriented contest, where TSR's from both teams earn the right to shoot at a real toy basketball hoop from two- or three-point range, depending on calling performance.

Material/Supplies Needed:

- Toy basketball hoop and ball

- Whistle

Contest Goal: To increase sales.

Duration: One day or shift.

Contest Rules/Guidelines: Divide your people into two teams. Assign a team coach (to act as cheerleader). Reaching individual productivity goals earns attempts at three-point baskets or two-point baskets (You might want to make the three-point shooting distance slightly farther, just like real basketball). Any written mistake on an order, or incorrect presentation is considered a foul, and the opposing team is awarded two free throws. Break time or lunch hour is half time. Equip supervisors with a whistle for fouls. An MVP can be chosen and awarded a special prize (or small trophy). Also choose a team prize such as pizza, soft drinks for all, tickets to an actual game, etc.

(45. TSR Basketball, continued)

Special Tips For Success: Have supervisors wear black and white striped shirts to act as referees. Run the contest in conjunction with a big local pro or college game.

Great contest for generating team focus on a goal. Dave Worman

46. Mystery Contest

Contest Creator: Linda Weigle

Title: Inside Sales Supervisor

Company: Cleveland Cotton Products

Location: Cleveland, OH

Contest Description: TSR's will work at maximum levels, unaware of the calling goal for the day. At shift's end, a ticket that identifies the call objective is drawn from a hat. Whoever met that objective for the day wins!

Material/Supplies Needed: Hat, or other creative container; strips of paper listing possible objectives for the day.

Contest Goal: To vary the goals and keep the reps on their toes!

Duration: One-two weeks.

Contest Rules/Guidelines: Each TSR works the day not knowing which goal will be chosen at the end of the day. They spread their emphasis that way, not focusing on one skill only for the contest. This can be used to emphasis cross-selling, up-selling, new items, new customers, most calls per day, most sales per day, etc. A daily prize is awarded. The size of the prize is based on budget. I like the effect of immediately awarding prizes at the end of each day.

Special Tips For Success: Display the prizes or pictures of the prizes around the room to generate enthusiasm.

This contest keeps my inside sales representatives on their toes, because the contest doesn't emphasize any one goal, but puts emphasis on using all of their skills. Linda A. Weigle

47. Making Tracks Toward the Gold

Contest Creator: Susan T. Meyer

Title: President

Company: The Obermeyer Group, Limited

Location: Fort Collins, CO

Contest Description: Award your TSR's varying amounts of points for corresponding levels of achievement, and track the progress on a large grid that is visible to all. Motivational banners and signs increase the enthusiasm, which in turn increases the production.

Material/Supplies Needed:

- Large sheet of paper or a banner of paper.

- Energy to create motivating messages and signs (Or of course you can buy them).

Contest Goal: We're a personnel recruiting and placement firm, and in our office, the goal is to get the most total cumulative points earned by executing what we term "action calls," "send outs," "job orders," and "placements." Played through individual efforts or team efforts the ultimate goal is increased productivity which leads to increased revenues for the company.

Duration: Timing can vary. With high rewards, the time may be four-six weeks, or with lower-valued rewards, the time may be five-ten working days.

Contest Rules/Guidelines: Here's how we award points: action call = 1 point; send out = 10 points; job order = 5 points; placement = 100 points. A qualifying number of points is required to

(47. Making Tracks Toward the Gold, continued)

Contest Rules/Guidelines: *(continued)*

enter the competition (100 or 150 points work well). The highest number of points wins, whether it is for an individual or for a team. The points are plotted on grid, or squares are colored to illustrate progress. In our case, send outs (interviews) must be verified and job orders must meet a minimum criteria for points to be earned. Placements must be invoiced prior to the points being counted. Here's our prize structure: 1st prize = weekend for two at a hotel or resort, or a play and dinner, or an individualized prize for the winner. 2nd prize = dinner for two, movie passes with refreshments, and a gift certificate. During the contest, put up banners and motivational posters around the office. Also pay special attention to those who are really hustling; we give little tantalizing notes to motivate recruiters to dial more and to get more from each call. My experience has been that a natural competition springs up between recruiters resulting in even more production. We vary the contest by using only send outs and job orders, or it can be done with teams instead of individuals. The contest can be used to focus on an area in the office that is lagging behind like new recruits, new job orders, send outs or placements.

Special Tips for Success: Make it fun, fun, fun! The atmosphere should be festive, and all levels of recruiters should be encouraged to participate. Ample recognition of work in progress is also a key.

Intra-office competition fuels this contest's fire. Increased productivity numbers and long-term results are the rewards to an office that uses this contest. Susan T. Meyer

48. Dialing for (insert your company's name) Dollars

Contest Creator: Linda Weigle

Title: Inside Sales Supervisor

Company: Cleveland Cotton Products

Location: Cleveland, OH

Contest Description: Call objectives are associated with dollar values. Simulated cash builds up on your TSR's desks as they produce more for themselves and you. They use their phoney cash at the end of the contest to buy prizes, or cash in their fake money for real currency.

Material/Supplies Needed:

- Play money

- List of objectives to reach to earn or win the dollars

- Prizes

Contest Goal: The goal is to win money and cash it in at the end of the week or buy a prize with it at the end of the week. Naturally they need to increase their performance to do this.

Duration: Two weeks.

Contest Rules/Guidelines: A list of objectives with dollar values assigned to each is posted for all to see. The excitement builds as the dollars are passed out and stacked up at their desks as they meet those objectives. At the end of each week they can cash their

48. Dialing for (insert your company's name) Dollars, continued

Contest Rule/Guidelines: *(continued)*

fake bucks in for the real thing, or buy prizes with a sale price attached.

Special Tips For Success: To keep the prep time down for contests I use cash, which my people love!

The immediate enthusiasm this fun contest generates is amazing, and I am able to feel like a game show host.   Linda A. Weigle

49. Profit Pig

Contest Creator: Michelle Hall

Title: Senior Account Manager

Company: Mettam Safety Supply, Incorporated

Location: Danville, Illinois

Contest Description: Be a real "pig" when it comes to selling at the highest profit. This contest is ideal for business-to-business account reps who have the authority to adjust the prices at which they sell to their customers. Selling products at, or above, a targeted gross margin will earn your reps more money, which is displayed on a scoreboard. The higher the margin, the more they earn. The first rep to reach his/her individual goal and fill their scoreboard receives a grand prize.

Material/Supplies Needed:

- **Profit Pig** scoreboard for each account manager

- Daily invoice totals for each account manager

- Grand prize

Contest Goal: The object of the contest is to fill the **Profit Pig** scoreboard with as many "X's" as possible. Having an "X" on your scoreboard indicates you are selling products at least at the goal gross margin. The overall goal is to raise the company's amount of profitability. This contest makes us aware of at what gross margin percentages we are selling to our customers.

Duration: The duration of the contest is one month. It starts the fist billing (invoice) day of the month and lasts through the final billing day of the month chosen to run the contest.

(49. Profit Pig, continued)

Contest Rules/Guidelines: For each account manager to fill their scoreboard, you will need to review the orders that have been invoiced. 1) Review each line item on the invoice individually. 2) The line item must have a gross margin at or above the goal gross margin percentage. This percentage will differ depending on your company goals). 3) The total dollar amount of each line item sold must be a least a certain amount. We use the dollar amount of the total invoice that is breakeven for shipping the order to make a profit, $40.00. That means for our company each line item must equal $40.00 to count. 4) Each time you meet the above criteria, place an "X" on your scoreboard. 5) Back orders of stock items will count too, if the total of the line item shipped plus the back order meets the above criteria. Award the grand prize (and perhaps a stuffed animal **Profit Pig** as a trophy) to the first one to fill up his/her scoreboard.

Special Tips For Success: Before giving the price to a customer/prospect, encourage reps to check gross margins and quote prices that will get the order, plus meet the goal of the **Profit Pig** contest. Check invoices on a daily basis.

This contest creates bigger sales, better gross margins and lots of fun competing to be the first finished for the BIGGEST PRIZE!
Michelle Hall

50. Wheel of Fortune II

Contest Creator: Carole Cline

Title: Personnel Sales Manager

Company: Suarez Corporation

City: Canton, Ohio

Contest Description: You don't have to solve puzzles in this version of **Wheel of Fortune**. Meeting objectives earns spins, which result in prizes (if their spin is successful).

Material/Supplies Needed: Large poster board or wooden wheel that has to be able to spin, and must be sturdy to withstand the spins.

Contest Goal: To make a sale so they can spin the wheel.

Duration: One day or shift.

Contest Rules/Guidelines: In our environment, TSR's will get to spin the wheel once for a credit card sale, or for two sales by check. Arrange wheel with different cash prizes, or other merchandise prizes of some sort.

When the phone room is down in sales, or to create excitement, Wheel of Fortune is a big morale booster. Spinning the wheel creates excitement for sales. One spin determines their fate. Carole Cline

51. Red "O" (Order) Contest

Contest Creator: Michelle Hall

Title: Senior Account Manager

Company: Mettam Safety Supply, Incorporated

Location: Danville, Illinois

Contest Description: This is another way to use the machine you will have if you play Contest 6, **The Gumball Contest.** In this one, sales will earn TSR's pennies to put in the gumball machine which is filled with multi-colored gumballs, but only one coveted white gumball. They try to collect the red gumballs, which are the only ones worth money. The ultimate prize will be awarded to the lucky person getting the white one. Remember, don't accidentally chew your profits away.

Material/Supplies Needed:

- One gum ball machine

- Enough multi-colored gumballs to fill the machine, including red gumballs; one white gumball (pennies are supplied by the account managers)

Contest Goal: The objective of the contest is to get outbound orders. By doing so, the account managers get chances at putting pennies in the gumball machine to collect the white gumball or the red gumballs.

Duration: Until all red gumballs and the white gumballs are gone. Usually 2-4 weeks.

Contest Rules/Guidelines: For each outbound order, defined as an order which the account manager initiates by calling the

(51. Red "O" (Order) Contest, continued)

Contest Rules/Guidelines *(continued)***:**

customer/prospect and actually taking the order over the phone within the eight-hour work shift, the account manager gets a chance to put a penny in the gumball machine to receive a gumball. Each red gumball is worth $5.00. These red gumballs are collected for the week and paid off at the end of each week. All other gumballs are worth only the price of a gumball and no money is given to them, with the exception of the single white gumball. The white gumball is worth $50.00 and is paid instantly upon receiving it out of the gumball machine. It is important to note while collecting the red gumballs, do not eat them! Inbound orders, defined as a customer/prospect calling in to the account manager, do not count in this contest unless the account manger has first called the customer/prospect, who is in turn calling back the same day to place an order. This order would not count if they called in the next day.

Special Tips For Success: Encourage reps to ALWAYS ASK FOR THE ORDER!

This contest is great success; it creates a high energy level, anticipating who will get the next order and ultimately who will get the BIG MONEY! Michelle Hall

52. Steak and Beans

Contest Creator: Carole Cline

Title: Personnel Sales Manager

Company: Suarez Corporation

Location: Canton, Ohio

Contest Description: Two teams compete for a week to determine who will dine on steak at week's end, and who will have to eat beans. Daily sales-per-hour is visibly posted to keep both teams up to date on the status of the contest.

Material/Supplies Needed: Each member of the winning team receives two strip steaks; the losing team members each get a can of pork and beans.

Contest Goal: The team with the highest sales dollar-per-hour wins, or the team with the highest credit card sales.

Duration: One week.

Contest Rules/Guidelines: Split TSR's into two teams. Select team captains. Post sales results daily. Choose team names, for example, Hot Potatos vs. Corn Cobs, etc. Choose team colors and decorate.

Special Tips For Success: Add filet migon steaks to the top two TSR's on each team to increase sales. A variation of this contest would be to have the losing team actually cook the steak dinner for the winners at a barbeque.

A sizzling contest for summer months. The contest heats up performance! Carole Cline

53. Survival

Contest Creator: Frank H. Feldhaus III

Title: Manager

Company: Gannett Telemarketing Incorporated

City: Cincinnati, Ohio

Contest Description: A large board is divided into squares representing the number of TSR's working that day. Each TSR is secretly assigned to a square by management. As TSR's reach calling goals, they go up and choose a square, therefore "killing" their opponents, and possibly winning prizes. The sole survivor wins the grand prize.

Material/Supplies Needed: Poster board, markers, grand prize.

Contest Goal: To be the last survivor. The winner receives the top prize.

Duration: One shift.

Contest Rules/Guidelines: Start by squaring off the poster board into blocks similar to a battleship grid. Then draw a copy of the board on a sheet of paper to act as the master. On the master, assign each TSR a square. You can hide money or prizes behind certain squares. Depending on your office size, you can have your TSR's come to the board every sale or every designated number or dollar volume of sales. The game itself: When reps hit their goal they come to the grid and place an "X" on any square. Anyone who is assigned that square is killed. If you're killed, you can still come to the board and play, but you won't be the last survivor of course. The rep could also win a prize hidden behind the square. The game continues until there is one last survivor.

(53. Survival, continued)

Special Tips For Success: Instigate friendly animosity by teasing the ones who are killed to get revenge, which they can do by getting sales to kill off the one who got them.

The survival game always increases productivity due to the fact everyone wants to be spotlighted when they hit their goal.
Frank Feldhaus III

54. Little League

Contest Creator: Frank H. Feldhaus III

Title: Manager

Company: Gannett Telemarketing, Incorporated

Location: Cincinnati, Ohio

Contest Description: TSR's are divided into two baseball teams. Small baseballs (or cutouts of baseballs) with different offensive values written on them are dumped in a baseball helmet. When goals are met, a TSR pulls out a baseball and the action is determined by the value of the ball: out, single, double, triple, home run. Track results on large poster board baseball diamonds.

Material/Supplies Needed:

- Baseball helmet to use as a bucket

- Small novelty baseball erasers, or simply pieces of paper

- Marker board

Contest Goal: To increase performance and build team unity.

Duration: One day or shift.

Contest Rules/Guidelines: Draw two baseball diamonds on marker board, or use cardboard and pushpins. Label the baseballs as follows: three of the balls with an "S " (single); two balls "D" (double); one ball "T" (triple); and one ball "HR" (home run). Mark the remaining balls with "O" (out). Divide the room into two teams. For every sale, reps pull a ball out of the bucket. If they get a hit, you mark it down. The game is all offense; in other words, it doesn't matter if you get three outs —

(54. Little League, continued)

Contest Rules/Guidelines: *(continued)*

your team still plays. There are no innings. The game is over when the shift ends. You can reward most hits, RBI's, even the home run champ. Prizes should be baseball-related.

Special Tips For Success: Great contest for Opening Day and World Series time. Have a baseball atmosphere, serve root beer, popcorn, cracker jacks or hot dogs to build the fun!

Everyone secretly wants to win the game for their team, so they're all trying harder. Sales increases are guaranteed!
Frank H. Feldhaus III

55. A Day at the Races

Contest Creator: Dave Worman

Title: Manager of Corporate Telemarketing

Company: Diebold, Incorporated

City: Canton, Ohio

Contest Description: TSR's bet on each other regarding who the top producing people will be for that day. To stimulate performance, each TSR must include themselves in their own bet. In order to win, their three guesses must be correct. Grand prize(s) are awarded to anyone guessing them in order (Win, Place, Show).

Material/Supplies Needed: NONE, other than prizes.

Contest Goal: Placing the proper bets and increasing your sales.

Duration: One day or shift.

Contest Rules/Guidelines: At the beginning of the shift, each rep bets on who the top three reps of the day will be. They bet to Win, Place, and Show. Each rep must include themselves in the top three bets. First prize: the rep who guesses the top three reps correctly and in the right order. Second prize: the reps who correctly predicted their own top three finish. Third prize: goes to *all* the reps who guessed one of the top three finishes.

Special Tips For Success: 1st, 2nd, and 3rd place ribbons in addition to prizes.

Seems to always tap into that energy we all have. Dave Worman

56. Grab Bag II

Contest Creator: Frank H. Feldhaus III

Title: Manager

Company: Gannett Telemarketing, Incorporated

City: Cincinnati, Ohio

Contest Description: A fixed number of grocery bags filled with mystery objects are stapled shut to be given out on the hour. Reaching goals each hour earns the TSR's a ticket for each drawing. Names are drawn and **Grab Bags** are awarded or chosen.

Material/Supplies Needed: Ask your reps to bring in "stuff" from their attics, basements, etc. Obtain grocery bags about ten days in advance.

Contest Goal: To meet objectives and win a bag.

Duration: One day or shift, all the way to one week.

Contest Rules/Guidelines: Fill five grocery bags with the items the reps have brought in and staple them shut. Then for every sale, or number of sales, put the rep's name in a bucket. Every hour, or one per shift, draw a name out, and that rep wins whatever bag they wish.

The fun isn't in winning something valuable, but seeing the strange things filling the bag! Frank Feldhaus III

57. Turkey Bowl

Contest Creator: Carole Cline

Title: Personnel Sales Manager

Company: Suarez Corporation

City: Canton, Ohio

Contest Description: Very simple and most effective around Thanksgiving and Christmas. Two teams of TSR's compete for the highest sales-per-hour, with winners receiving a coupon for a turkey.

Material/Supplies Needed: Gift certificate for turkey for the winning team members. For the losing team, give out some type of hoiday-related gift.

Contest Goal: To get the most sales and be the winning team, and receive a gift certificate for a turkey.

Duration: One week.

Contest Rules/Guidelines: Divide phone room into two teams. Pick team captains for coaches. The team with the highest sales dollar-per-hour wins.

Special Tips For Success: Run contest for Thanksgiving or Christmas. Decorate with team colors.

Is a great holiday contest during Thanksgiving and football season.
Carole Cline

58. Surfin' USA

Contest Creator: Dave Worman

Title: Manager of Corporate Telemarketing

Company: Diebold, Incorporated

Location: Canton,OH

Contest Description: A beach-themed contest. TSR's try to earn coconut pieces by reaching performance goals. Most pieces at end of day win. Creating an authentic atmosphere and adding a little music highlights this popular event.

Material/Supplies Needed:

- Beach cut-outs and other affiliated props (If you're real adventurous, bring some sand in)

- Beach Boys and Jan & Dean tapes or records

- Hawaiian leis, pineapples, coconuts

Contest Goal: To increase productivity while having a fun day at the beach.

Duration: One day or shift.

Contest Rules/Guidelines: EVERYONE dresses accordingly with Hawaiian shirts, clamdiggers, leis, sandals, etc. By reaching goals, a TSR receives a certain number of fresh cut coconut pieces. Different performance levels should equal different amounts of coconut points. At break, play bits of songs by the Beach Boys or Jan & Dean. Correctly guessing record titles earns

(58. Surfin' USA, continued)

Contest Rules/Guidelines: *(continued)*

TSR's extra coconut points. Most coconut points at shift's end wins. Award 2nd and 3rd place as well.

Special Tips for Success: Have theme prizes such as tickets to a water park, sunglasses, etc. Don't get hungry and eat any of your coconut bites!

Everyone wins here. A fun atmosphere, especially with additional production and theme prizes. A great time! Dave Worman

59. 40K Run

Contest Creator: Teri Mass

Title: Direct Manager, Line Advertising

Company: PennySaver

Location: Vista, CA

Contest Description: This telemarketing marathon begins with an average base number of weekly sales for each of two teams. Increasing sales over that base number each week is the goal and will advance you "X" number of miles in the race. The first team to make 40 sales over the base number wins.

Material/Supplies Needed:

- Art work of runners (or horses) to display progress.

- Cash bonus (1st, 2nd, 3rd places).

Contest Goal: To increase sales over last month.

Duration: One month.

Contest Rules/Guidelines: 1) Teams of two are created by department manager. 2) Determine base number or average sales of team from previous month as a starting point for each team. 3) Each team's goal is to increase sales over that base number. 4) Results are measured weekly so runners can advance one mile for each $100 increase weekly (Dollar amount may vary. We are a weekly publication so all our results are weekly, but any time period may be used.) 5) Department manager displays progress as runners advance miles. Finish line is 40 increments (average of 10 per week) and should be able to have a winner in four weeks or less. 6) Cash prizes for 1st place, 2nd place and 3rd place to

(59. 40K Run, continued)

Contest Rules/Guidelines: *(continued)*

each team member. (Note: If adapting to horses, offer trip to races for the winners.)

Special Tips for Success: Keep the contest visual! Base remains unchanged so the teams do not have to beat the previous week's results; they only have to beat base. For us this contest rewards long-term contracts, because one four-week ad will help every week of the contest, instead of having to make a new sale each week.

A fun inspiration to build on those sales we have, and adds incremental business. A great contest to track benefits from multiple sales or contract sales. Teri Maas

60. The Company Picnic

Contest Creator: Susan T. Meyer

Title: President

Company: The Obermeyer Group, Limited

Location: Fort Collins, CO

Contest Description: The office works as a team to determine the food for the company picnic. A large visible thermometer is posted with pictures of hot dogs at the bottom climbing to filet mignon and lobster at the top. Reaching specific calling goals moves the team up the food ladder until the contest ends. The TSR's determine if they fast or feast!

Material/Supplies Needed: Grid to follow points earned, and the food for the picnic.

Contest Goal: A team effort to determine what type of picnic fixins' the company will provide during a company picnic. The goal of the participants is to earn enough points to have steak and lobster provided instead of hot dogs and hamburgers. The goals for the Company are to increase activity within the office to bring in more revenue.

Duration: Two or three weeks work well, or a longer period of time can be successful.

Contest Rules/Guidelines: All reps participate as equals while accumulating points. The points are recorded on a thermometer-type grid which plainly shows progress toward the various types of foods to be provided at the picnic. At the bottom of the thermometer are no-name hot dogs followed by Ball Park Franks (they plump up when you cook them), all beef patties, chopped

(60. The Company Picnic, continued)

Contest Rules/Guidelines: *(continued)*

sirloin, round steak, chuck steak, T-bones, filet mignons, and, finally at the top of the thermometer, filet mignon with lobster tails. Wherever the points earned ends is the type of entree the company must provide for the company picnic. The points required to eat filet and lobster is set relatively high; the office must really stretch to earn such delights. If you are in a small office, then the points are allocated accordingly. Long term residual of increased production can be realized from this contest.

Special Tips for Success: The prize must be something everyone wants to work for and to generate excitement.

A total office effort that combines hard work with great fun. For us this contest gives increased telephone and personal interviews as well as job orders. It also is easily adapted to Christmas parties and other events. Susan T. Meyer

61. Wizard of Oz's Emerald City Contest

Contest Creator: Carole Cline

Title: Personnel Sales Manager

Company: Suarez Corporation

Location: Canton, Ohio

Contest Description: A Wizard of Oz theme contest. Which team can make it to the Emerald City first? Hitting performance goals will move your team along the yellow brick road, encountering all the Oz characters along the way.

Material/Supplies Needed: Large poster with yellow brick road; story characters: Dorothy, Scarecrow, Tin Man, Lion and Wizard of Oz.

Contest Goal: To be the team with the highest sales dollar per hour each week, and receive an emerald piece of jewelry in electroplate or sterling silver.

Duration: Four weeks. The month of May ties in nicely, since the emerald is the birthstone for May.

Contest Rules/Guidelines: TSR's are divided into two teams according to working hours so each team is balanced. Team names are: Dorothy and Toto vs. Munchkins. Establish performance goals, and the length of the Yellow Brick Road the teams will move for accomplishing the goals. Prizes are awarded each week to the first team to reach the (characters on the poster wall) Scarecrow, 1st week; Tin Man, 2nd week; Lion, 3rd week; Wizard of Oz, 4th week. Have a covered-dish pot luck luncheon, and have a costume party the 4th week. Give cash prizes for the best costume and the most creative green covered food dish.

(61. Wizard of Oz's
Emerald City Contest, continued)

Special Tips For Success: This contest is great for May because of emerald being May's birthstone.

Maximizes sales and profit. Carole Cline

62. Become a Telephone Sales Expert

Contest Creator: Mary Gill

Title: Telemarketing Manager

Company: Advance Business Systems and Supply Company

City: Cockeysville, Maryland

Contest Description: A telemarketing seminar is the grand prize awaiting the individual that becomes the telephone sales expert for the month. Appropriate quotas are distributed and points are awarded for achievement. Highest point totals for the month wins and attends the seminar.

Material/Supplies Needed: Flyers to hand out.

Contest Goal: Increase telemarketing productivity in their individual territories.

Duration: One month/23 working days.

Contest Rules/Guidelines: For us, quota is figured as 23 working days times one demonstration per day, or 23 demonstrations. The top rep with the most points wins and attends the seminar.

Telemarketers get paid with time off, and their new skills help increase personal production as well as furthering departmental goals. One Telemarketer is designated to bring back the information presented in the seminar, and give a mini seminar at lunch time to their department. The entire work force wins the contest this way.
Mary Gill

63. Beat Your Own Record

Contest Creator: Susan McConnell

Title: Director of Sales

Company: South Hills Data Comm

Location: Pittsburg, PA

Contest Description: TSR's compete against themselves as they attempt to BEAT their own record. Use average sales-per-rep as a benchmark, and then run this contest for a month or more. Affiliate certain percentage increases with specific dollar values and watch each person roll up their sleeves and go to work!

Material/Supplies Needed: Reps with the will to succeed.

Contest Goal: Productivity gains in outbound calling over a long period.

Duration: One-three months.

Contest Rules/Guidelines: Take average number of daily outbound presentations of each rep; set a bonus amount if productivity grows at a set percent. For example, 25% or higher = $150 bonus; 20-24% = $100 bonus; 15-19% = $50 bonus.

Special Tips for Success: Have an awards banquet with upper management recognition for productivity gains.

This contest has increased outbound presentations from 5% to 20%. Results vary from rep to rep, but productivity remains at the higher level after the contest is over. Susan McConnell

64. Keys for Selling

Contest Creator: Jeannette Fannin

Title: Director, Sales and Marketing

Company: Hardware Sales Company

Location: Cordova, TN

Contest Description: TSR's earn keys by reaching goals. At the end of the contest all keys are dumped into a bin and a certain number are drawn for prizes.

Material/Supplies Needed: One large treasure box for display and individual treasure boxes filled with candy goodies.

Contest Goal: Get a lot of keys to increase chance of winning prize at end of contest.

Duration: One week.

Contest Rules/Guidelines: Each telephone account manager receives an initial treasure box filled with candy goodies. Each sale receives a numbered key to put in his/her treasure box. (By this time our TSR's had eaten their goodies then were eating our candy gold coins used in the display!) As the TSR puts their key into their treasure box, they log the number written on the back of the key. At the end of the contest each TSR dumps their treasure box of keys into a bin for a grand prize drawing. The more sales, the more keys, and the better the chance of winning! The winning number is drawn .... but, wait! Everyone is a winner. Consolation prizes are drawn until everyone has won something.

Keys For Selling started our TSR's on one of the most positive and productive sales campaigns ever! Jeannette Fannin

65. Valentine Incentive

Contest Creator: Lori Bradish

Title: Inside Sales Manager

Company: Schneider Communications, Incorporated

Location: Green Bay, WI

Contest Description: Management fills a large Valentine box with Valentines that have prizes written on the back of some. Reaching calling goals awards a TSR the opportunity to choose a Valentine and hopefully a prize.

Material/Supplies Needed: Children's Valentines, candy kisses, money or gift certificates, and time off.

Contest Goal: To increase sales.

Duration: First two weeks of February.

Contest Rules/Guidelines: We fill a box with the valentines. On the back of some valentines we write a prize. We give out 1/2 hours off, $2, $5, $10, or candy kisses. The reps can pick a valentine every time they get a sale.

A great way to spark the results during the winter doldrums.
Lori Bradish

66. The House That (Name of TSR) Built

Contest Creator: Linda Weigle

Title: Inside Sales Supervisor

Company: Cleveland Cotton Products

Location: Cleveland, OH

Contest Description: By reaching appropriate calling goals, TSR's slowly build their own house piece by piece on a poster board. As each one finishes they receive a prize.

Material/Supplies Needed: Poster board

Contest Goal: To build a house within two weeks. The bricks, chimney, door, windows and bushes.

Duration: Two weeks.

Contest Rules/Guidelines: To build your house, you're given your posterboard and a list of objectives that will earn you a brick, for example, an add-on sale wins you two bricks; for an increased order you win a window. Dispense the bricks, etc., after each objective. Also have a couple of real special goals to win the chimney and door! This can be tailor made to the quantities you're after. Finally, each telesales rep who finishes their house wins a prize. This can be cash or actual prizes. I find our reps work best in less competitive environments like this.

Involve your salespeople in the contest concept; it increases their excitement. We experienced an 86% increase in add-on sales by giving a brick for each additional add-on sold. Another reason it was so successful is our whole inside sales department participated in designing this contest. Linda A. Weigle

67. $uccess Desk

Contest Creator: Brenda Watts

Company: TeleWatts Market Services

Location: Toronto, Ontario, Canada

Contest Description: Winning this contest will get you two weeks at the very visible $uccess desk. TSR's compete to reach calling goals that will set them up for the win.

Material/Supplies Needed: Overhanging $uccess sign, lavishly decorated office or cubicle.

Contest Goal: TSR with top sales/leads wins use of $uccess desk for two weeks!

Duration: Rotating two week intervals.

Contest Rules/Guidelines: Goals set and separately issued depending on which TSR's are working on what client projects. Punctuality/reliability taken into consideration.

Help them to know what $uccess feels like.   Brenda Watts

68. Trick or Treat

Contest Creator: Dave Worman

Title: Manager of Corporate Telemarketing

Company: Diebold, Incorporated

Location: Canton, Ohio

Contest Description: This is a Halloween version of the **Who, What, or Where Poster Board**, with a few twists. TSR's achieving appropriate calling goals choose black or orange candy from a pumpkin, which then determines which poster he/she may try to unmask (celebrity poster with self sticking notes covering the identity). Some notes may have TREATS (time off, money, etc) on the back and some may have TRICKS (must sing a song, tell a joke, etc.). Identifying posters wins grand prizes.

Material/Supplies Needed: Plastic pumpkin, celebrity posters, self sticking notes, Halloween candy.

Contest Goal: To have some Halloween fun while increasing sales orders.

Duration: One day or shift.

Contest Rules/Guidelines: For reaching calling goals, TSR's will pick from a large plastic pumpkin filled with candy wrapped in orange or black paper. The color of the wrapper determines from which poster board the TSR may now choose a self sticking note. The stickers act as a mask covering the poster of a famous person, and also have either a trick or a treat on the opposite side. Tricks must sing a song or tell a joke to everyone prior to the next shift. Treats can be a 1/2 hour break or a dollar amount. A TSR chooses a note by pulling it from the poster board, thus removing part of

(68. Trick or Treat, continued)

Contest Rules/Guidelines *(continued)*:

the mask. He/she checks the back of the tag to find out whether they got tricked or treated, and they also then guess the identity of the person(s) behind the mask.   Whoever identifies the mystery person on each board wins $13.00.

Special Tips For Success: Encourage your staff to wear Halloween costumes (that don't interfere with their job) and have a costume-judging competition at break time.   Winner gets additional draws from the posters.

Always scares up some additional sales orders. Dave Worman

69. Confuscious Say

Contest Creator: Sandra Fava

Title: Promotion Coordinator

Company: NEBS

Location: Groton, MA

Contest Description: Teams compete for top sales to receive envelopes with Chinese proverbs and possible prizes enclosed. Daily prizes are awarded, and a Chinese luncheon or dinner awaits the ultimate winning team with the most sales.

Material/Supplies Needed:

- Chinese food take out boxes

- Fortune cookie sayings in gift enclosure envelopes

- "Confuscious say . . . . " tickets.

Contest Goal: To generate additional sales for the department, to increase the number of sales on certain products, and to have some fun within the department.

Duration: Two-four weeks.

Contest Rules/Guidelines: Our department was divided into teams. Each team was given a packet which explained the promotion strategy and procedure. We included samples of the products we were promoting, scripts for selling, tickets to track sales information and a Chinese food box for the group. Every time a sales rep sold one of the promotion products, they would complete the information on the ticket and drop it into their group's Chinese Box. Sales were tallied daily. The top selling group for

(69. Confuscious Say, continued)

Contest Rules/Guidelines *(continued)*:

the day was given enough Chinese sayings for everyone in the group. The sayings were handed out in sealed gift enclosure envelopes. One envelope contained a $10.00 certificate to a local Chinese restaurant. Everyday someone won a prize! At the end of the promotion the group who averaged the highest number of sales was treated to a Chinese luncheon.

Special Tips For Success: The department was decorated with Chinese symbols and cut outs which added to the fun.

Great for creating a spirit of healthy competition! Sandra Fava

70. Indy 500

Contest Creator: Tim Lybrook

Title: President - Consultant

Company: Marketing Services Unlimited

Location: Bloomington, IN

Contest Description: Ladies and gentlemen . . . . start your engines! Individual TSR's qualify and compete for pole position by reaching appropriate calling goals set by management. Follow the actual race on a large poster board race track with construction paper cars named by each TSR.

Material/Supplies Needed:

- Colored paper for race cars
- Markers
- Five-eight sheets of white poster board to make track
- Race flags to put around the room

Contest Goal: To finish the race the fastest. Depending on number of telemarketers, prizes may be given to first place only, top three finishes, or the top five.

Duration: One-three weeks, depending on what your goals are.

Contest Rules/Guidelines: Each telemarketer cuts a race car out of the colored paper and puts a car name on it. Being creative with the name adds to the fun. Draw a large track on the white posterboard and post it on the wall. It should include start-finish line, spectators, race flags, etc. The track should be placed where

(70. Indy 500, continued)

Contest Rules/Guidelines *(continued)*:

everyone can see it. Tape all cars to the start-finish line. When contest begins, cars are moved a certain number of spaces around the track, depending on pre-set criteria. Could be one space per appointment or sale, two spaces for something you really need extra effort on, and three spaces for a really outstanding achievement. Use the spaces to your advantage. To make the contest more exciting, you can have qualifications and see who should start in which space. Prizes can be awarded for first car to complete one lap, or 10 laps, or whatever you'd like to do. Post the standings each day. Use your imagination for prizes. For example, first place could be a trophy with a race car attached, and/or cash, or whatever you come up with. You can do some creative things with car-related items, such as gift certificates to auto accessory stores, tire and lube places, etc.

Really puts people in the racing spirit. They were constantly go, go, go! Tim Lybrook

71. The Massage

Contest Creator: Christopher A. Jacobs, Ph.D., E. E.

Title: President

Company: Jacobs Electronics

Location: Midland, TX

Contest Description: The first TSR reaching appropriate calling goals is greeted by a professional masseuse who remains with them until another TSR reaches the goal. The masseuse then works on the next winner as everyone tries to make the next sale.

Material/Supplies Needed: A willing individual with good, strong hands to be the masseuse (A trained professional will work best), and motivated telemarketers.

Contest Goal: To continue to make the "most recent sale" so they will be the recipient of a professional massage. Massage constitutes a back rub and shoulder massage.

Duration: Four hours.

Contest Rules/Guidelines: We hire a professional masseuse to come in for four hours. The telemarketer who makes the last sale gets a massage . . . . up until another telemarketer makes a sale — the most recent sale always gets the massage. The telemarketer who made the most recent sale and therefore earned the massage can stop phoning customers if he/she desires while they are enjoying it. But most don't because they want to keep the massage going by making the most recent sale.

(71. The Massage, continued)

Special Tips For Success: In our group, what really increases motivation is when the masseuse is an attractive woman, since most of our telemarketers are men.

Enthusiasm picks up significantly when the masseuse enters the room, especially if the masseuse comes equipped with all kinds of body oils and has an enthusiastic, friendly demeanor. Any TSR who might have been on a smoke or dinner break will come bounding into the salesroom, pick up their lead book, and immediately get on the phone. This high-visibility, big prestige reward results not only in feeling good, but also produces a super-charged, high energy rivalry in the room, enhanced when the masseuse calls out the name of the next winning TSR. Chris Jacobs

72. Envelopes

Contest Creator: Anne Betts

Title: New Products Administrator

Company: Control-O-Fax Systems, Incorporated

Location: Waterloo, IA

Contest Description: At the beginning of the contest, each rep gets four sealed envelopes. When specific goals set by management are reached, they open an envelope. The value of the envelopes increase with each goal.

Material/Supplies Needed: Envelopes, prizes and labels.

Contest Goal: Motivate sales people to achieve special goals.

Duration: As long as it takes to hit objective.

Contest Rules/Guidelines: Give all telephone sales reps four envelopes. Each envelope is opened as an objective is met. For example, our company wanted to introduce a new file folder system to our customers. Therefore, people were able to open the first envelope the first time they probed for needs with a customer regarding this product. The second envelope after their first label sale. The third envelope was earned with the first folder sale. They opened their fourth envelope with their first $100.00 sold in filing. Enclosed in our envelopes: Fouth envelope, $50; third envelope, microwave popcorn; second envelope, candy bar; first envelope, $2.00.

Special Tips For Success: Make the first prize easily attainable to generate excitement. Another way to add mystery to the contest is to have a variety of different prizes for each category, so

(72. Envelopes, continued)

Contest Rules/Guidelines *(continued)*:

that reps would never know what was in their envelope until they opened it. For example, if you have 15 reps, you would have four groups of 15 envelopes each, with a variety of prizes. At the beginning of the contest, instead of handing out the envelopes, let them pick their own out of the pile.

This is a fun contest. Everyone likes to be a winner and everyone feels like a winner since the first objective doesn't involve a sale. It merely starts the sales process and overcomes the call reluctance that goes with presenting a new product to the customer. As envelopes are opened, TSR's seek out winners and share success techniques. Not only does the TSR learn but so do the trainers. Anne Betts

73. Business Card Incentive

Contest Creator: Brenda Mulder

Title: Sales Supervisor

Company: K-Products, Incorporated

Location: Orange City, IA

Contest Description: As goals are met by TSR's, they put their own business card in a large drum that is visible to all. Card drawings produce prize winners both short-term and long-term.

Material/Supplies Needed: System for tracking progress/business cards.

Contest Goal: To achieve monthly, quarterly and yearly goals set for each sales rep.

Duration: One year.

Contest Rules/Guidelines: A large drum currently resides in the middle of the TeleSales department. Each quarter a goal review meeting is held. At this time, the reps drop one business card into the drum for every goal they have met. At the yearly banquet in the fall, one card will be drawn from the drum. The winning rep will have a choice of a "Fun in the Sun" weekend in Arizona or a ski trip to Colorado.

Special Tips For Success: Make the first prize easily attainable to generate excitement.

(73. Business Card Incentive, continued)

It is motivating for the Reps to be able to drop their business cards in the drum and having their peers recognize the individuals achievement. What we found to help motivate the Reps was to have the progress chart centrally located. The Reps were able to see where everyone was and encouraged each other. Brenda Mulder

74. Treasure Map

Contest Creator: Barbara Burns

Title: President

Company: Burns and Associates

Location: Concordville, PA

Contest Description: This is more of a self-motivational tool than a contest. TSR's cut out magazine pictures that represent their own personal short-term and long-term goals (Furniture, car, vacation, etc.). Their Treasure Map of goals is posted in their area for everday view. Small prizes can accompany reaching calling goals, but the real motivation is ongoing . . . . their personal goals.

Material/Supplies Needed: Poster board, magazine pictures, marker.

Contest Goal: Set personal goals to help meet calling goals

Duration: Their lifetime.

Contest Rules/Guidelines: Have reps write down personal goals (near and ten-year goals). Cut out pictures from magazines that represent or symbolize that goal. Every morning before they pick up the phone to call, encourage them to look into the mirror, then look at the goal, visualizing themself being the image that the picture represents. They can have many goals . . . . from new furniture, car, vacation, house, money or other physical, spiritual or mental goals. This way, the power generated by company, project and personal focus can reach the company, project and personal goals. This motivation technique is on-going. Pin their Treasure Maps in front of them (next to their mirror) to remind

(74. Treasure Map, continued)

Contest Rules/Guidelines *(continued)*:

them why they're calling—what they personally will get from doing a good job for the company is up to them.

Special Tips For Success: My ABC's of success are: Attitude, Belief, Concentration, Desire, Effort and Focus . . . . leading us to our goals!

This is long-term motivation. The more success they have with obtaining their picture goals, the more they succeed at placing winning calls for the company. Barbara Burns

75. Football Hero

Contest Creator: Frank H. Feldhaus III

Title: Manager

Company: Gannett Telemarketing, Incorporated

Location: Cincinnati, Ohio

Contest Description: Similar to **Little League**, two teams will take to the gridiron and select small footballs from a helmet when reaching appropriate goals set by management. These footballs will have specific offensive action written on them (15 yards, fumble, TD, etc.) and it is tracked on a large poster board resembling a field. Highest score wins!

Material/Supplies Needed:

- Bucket (helmet)

- Twenty-five rubber footballs (small eraser footballs bought at novelty store)

- Marker

- Board or piece of cardboard drawn to resemble a football.

Contest Goal: The winning team gets the choice of prizes.

Duration: One shift.

Contest Rules/Guidelines: Label the footballs (or something similar) with "Pass +5," "Pass +10," "Pass +15," "Run +5," "Run +10," "Run +15," "Run -5," "Run -10," and "Run -15." Also mix in a couple of "no gains," "incompletes," and two "touchdowns" used for instant touchdowns. Divide the room into

(75. Football Hero, continued)

Contest Rules/Guidelines *(continued)*:

two teams, and for every sale the rep will pull a play out of the bucket. (Also keep track of individual gains/losses for prizes.) Both teams start on the twenty-yard line and move when their players get sales. Game ends when shift is over. Award prizes that are football related: sweatshirts, tee-shirts, hats, and posters. Award the winning team players. (Example, most yards gained, etc.)

Special Tips For Success: Hold this game during football season when a good match-up is on — especially on Monday Night Football.

This game helps reps encourage each other to sell to help their team, thus building confidence. Frank H. Feldhaus III

76. Two Dollar Special

Contest Creator: Carole Cline

Title: Personnel Sales Manager

Company: Suarez Corporation

Location: Canton, Ohio

Contest Description: TSR's earn $2 bills and visible gold stars on their way to a monthly grand prize.

Material/Supplies Needed: A stack of $2 bills.

Contest Goal: Management sets a sales goal per hour. TSA to reach their sales goal on a daily basis will receive a $2 bill.

Duration: Daily contest.

Contest Rules/Guidelines: Set a goal for the promotion they're calling or pertaining to what they are selling. Record daily goal winners with their name on a poster board for their co-workers to see. Place a gold star beside the name. TSA with the most gold stars beside their name in one month, gets cash award.

Special Tips For Success: Our TSA's collect two dollar bills.

Setting specific goals for the reps encourages the drive for sales. Meeting the goal with the cash award of two dollar bills makes it personally rewarding.   Carole Cline

77. Roll For Dollars Program

Contest Creator: Diane Johnston

Title: Telemarketing Supervisor

Company: Sandoz Nutrition Corporation

Location: Minneapolis, MN

Contest Description: TSR's opening new accounts or upselling existing customers will be awarded with rolls of the dice. Dollar volume determines the number of rolls, and points are associated with the number appearing on every roll of the dice. Points are totaled each week or month and turned into various gift certificates.

Material/Supplies Needed:

- Dice (2)

- Gift certificates

Contest Goal: To generate new account sales.

Duration: Rewards given monthly, but is an annual program.

Contest Rules/Guidelines: For each new account sold, or for each new product sold on an existing account, roll(s) of the dice are earned based on the dollar size of the order. The larger the sale, the more rolls are rewarded. Points (as rolled on the dice) are totalled monthly and gift certificates are awarded based on overall (point total) achievement. Follow-up/reorder rolls and points are also achieved the first time a reorder is received.

Special Tips For Success: Dice rolling and presentation of gift certificates are done at the weekly staff meeting in a group setting,

(77. Roll For Dollars Program, continued)

Special Tips For Success *(continued)*:

thus the recognition also serves as an excellent motivator in addition to the monetary reward.

We have been utilizing the Roll For Dollars Program in our department for three years and it continues to inspire excitement and motivation in the staff. The rolling of dice and acceptance of awards is done in a group setting, thus allowing for the sharing of successful sales strategies and group recognition. Diane Johnston

78. Build a Theater

Contest Creator: Dave Worman

Title: Manager of Corporate Telemarketing

Company: Diebold, Incorporated

Location: Canton, OH

Contest Description: The staff works as a team to reach calling goals to build the Theater. Magazine cut-outs represent all the equipment and headliners needed, and if completed before deadline (end of contest), opening night party is thrown for the office.

Material/Supplies Needed: Poster board, and cut-out pictures of station equipment (cameras, transmitters, display cases).

Contest Goal: Our goal was to increase credit card percentage and dollars sold per-hour.

Duration: One week, or designated time frame.

Contest Rules/Guidelines: The TSR's work as a team to buy equipment or shows for theater. Team must generate a predetermined amount of sales on credit cards for each item. To win, the theater must be totally equipped with gear and shows by deadline. Prize: Opening night party for group.

Special Tips For Success: Display all pictures of equipment. As team reaches goals, last person to get the credit card buys equipment and puts on poster board.

Promotes true team spirit as they all join together to reach the goal and have the party. Dave Worman

79. TGA Golf

Contest Creator: Dave Worman

Title: Manager of Corporate Telemarketing

Company: Diebold, Incorporated

Location: Canton, OH

Contest Description: Hitting appropriate performance goals allows TSR's to putt in front of everyone and compete for the trophy.

Material/Supplies Needed:

- Putt return device
- Putter
- Golf balls
- 15 x 2 ft. strip of green indoor/outdoor carpet.

Contest Goal: To increase sales.

Duration: One day or shift.

Contest Rules/Guidelines: For reaching goals a TSR gets to walk up the fairway to attempt a putt on the green. Each TSR chooses the length of putt to attempt:
15 ft. = EAGLE (-2 points)
12 ft. = BIRDIE (-1 point)
8 ft. = PAR (0 points)   If they miss any of these, *add* 1 point.

The TSR with the lowest score at shift's end wins.

(79. TGA Golf, continued)

Special Tips For Success: Managers, supervisors, and verifiers act as caddies for all TSR's, handing them the putter. Also, provide a trophy for winner.

Use this around the four major golf tournaments (U.S. Open, British Open, PGA Championship and the Masters), or at the time of a local PGA event for maximum enthusiasm. Dave Worman

A Final Note From Dave Worman

Congratulations!

You've reached the end of our journey, and are ready to proceed on to a series of exciting adventures . . . . adventures in the form of contests which will enhance the lives of the people who work for you, add more to the bottom line of your company, and make you look like a hero—in the eyes of your people, and your superiors.

You have exactly what you need to know in order to help your people reach new levels of accomplishment. You know:

- why contests work;

- which contests work best;

- how to time contests and set goals that motivate;

- what to give (and avoid) as prizes;

- specific tips which will ensure contest success;

- how to avoid post-contest letdown.

And of course, you have 79 actual contests you can use, or adapt in your own department today. Yes, everything you need to crank up the activity and enthusiasm by several decibels is right here in your hand.

Fortunately, our journey together need not end here. As a fellow telesales manager, I share with you the interest in finding new and exciting ways to motivate. It's a never-ending challenge. Therefore I invite you to stay in touch with me. It would be quite natural for us to create a sequel to this book, sharing more contests from experts like you who are testing out new ideas — and succeeding — every day. Give me your input on variations of ideas you try from this book, or contests you've created on your own.

Also, I'd be delighted to meet with you, and work with you in person. I frequently travel to telemarketing/telesales departments nationwide, rolling up my sleeves, digging in to motivational problems and implementing solutions that create explosions of positivism and increased performance. If you feel this might be appropriate at your organization, please call me.

Additionally, I also present these ideas at association meetings, sales meetings, and conventions. I'd love to talk with you about the possibilities, so again, I invite you to call.

Finally, I urge you, that with whatever degree you decide to implement the ideas we've covered in this book, keep one thing in mind: **enthusiasm is infectious!** *You* must have it for your people to have it.

Expand your imagination, be creative, and most of all, *have FUN!*

Thanks for joining me.

To contact Dave Worman, write or call:

D.L. Worman
P.O. Box 35213
North Canton, OH 44735
(216)499-7920

Here Are Other Ways You Can Help Your Employees and Make Your Job Easier

Business By Phone Inc., publishers of this book, specializes in resources to help organizations and individuals generate more sales and profits by phone. Here are some ways we might be able to help you.

Additional Copies of This Book, and Multiple Copy Discounts

If this is a borrowed copy, or if you want to get copies for all of your locations, as gifts, or for whatever reason, call us. We have multiple copy discounts to save you money. Or, for single copies, simply send your check, or credit card number, along with shipping information to the address on the next page.

Be Sure You're On The List To Be Notified of Future Updates to This Book

If you ordered this book by mail from us, you're on the list. If you picked it up elsewhere, you're out of luck regarding updates . . . . unless you register with us. Simply call or write our office and let us know you're a user of this book and want to be contacted with any further information.

Call the TELESALES TIPS LINE for Free Recorded Training Sessions

Each week you can provide your staff with a free mini training session on sales skills. Just have them call the Telesales Tips Line. They'll hear a recorded 3-5 minute message on sales skills, communication, or motivation. Some managers record the Tip and play it for their reps at meetings. Call it right now, and call regularly to take advantage of this FREE service. **(402)896-TIPS.**

Get A Free Subscription to the Business By Phone Training Products/Resources Catalog

This catalog details numerous books, audio tapes programs, videos, manuals, seminars and other items which can help you to train your people, and also ensure you put together and maintain a smoothly-running telesales/telemarketing department. Call to get on the list, and to get your free current copy.

Get the TELEPHONE SELLING REPORT Newsletter

Each month you'll get eight pages packed with to-the-point, what-to-say ideas for the people who are on the phone. You'll get word-for-word opening statements that generate interest, how to get to elusive decision makers, questions that help them buy, ways to answer tough objections, and many more. Call to get a sample copy today.